Betty Crocker's
COOKING WITH
WINE

Golden Press/New York
Western Publishing Company, Inc.
Racine, Wisconsin

Director of Photography: George Ancona
Illustrator: Murray Tinkelman

Second Printing in This Format, 1980

Printed in the U.S.A. by Western Publishing Company, Inc.
Published by Golden Press, New York, New York.
Library of Congress Catalog Card Number: 78-72939

Golden® and Golden Press® are trademarks of Western Publishing Company, Inc.

Contents

Dear Friend,

Whether you have always cooked with wine or have never uncorked a bottle, we invite you to enjoy this collection of tantalizing recipes, all of which have a touch of the grape. For the experienced we've assembled imaginative recipes to extend a repertoire; for the novice there are dishes, outstanding in flavor but simple to prepare, that will initiate you into the pleasures and techniques of cooking with wine.

Each recipe shows you how the use of wine enhances the savory, the subtle, the zesty or the delicate quality of the main ingredients. That's the unique talent of wine cookery; it makes the whole seem to be more than a sum of its parts!

The convenient red and white sections of the book will help you when you have a little leftover wine in a bottle and want to create something special. Often the difference between an ordinary casserole and a memorable main course is made with just a quarter cup of wine. Simply refer to the wine chart on page 8, which is organized with cooking in mind, for pointers on exactly what types of wine you'll need.

Because wine is a natural cooking ingredient all over the world, we've adapted a sampling of recipes from England, France, Russia, Greece, Germany and other countries to indicate how wine is used in various cuisines. In our own tradition we have a long history associated with wine—the first name of America, after all, was Vinland! In the last few years wine cookery has become widely popular in this country. No longer just for special occasions, but even for the preparation of soups, vegetables and desserts, cooks are discovering that wine has an invaluable place in their everyday cooking.

We're sure your adventures with these recipes will reward you, your family and friends with delicious memories.

Cheers!

Betty Crocker

A Few Facts About Wine

Cooking with Wine.
The reason to try it, if you haven't already, is simple. Wine has a particular talent for bringing out the finest taste and aroma in food. When wine is heated, the alcoholic content of the wine evaporates. Only the "essence" of the wine is left, to impart its richness and subtle flavor.

Be sure to use the quantity of wine suggested in the recipe and don't be tempted to splash in an extra half-cup. The secret of successful wine cookery depends on that perfect balance of ingredients.

The methods of using wine in food are simple: as a marinade, as part of the cooking liquid (poaching, simmering) or as a flavoring in uncooked foods such as desserts. Just be sure, when planning an entire menu, to include only one or two dishes that call for wine.

What Wine Should You Use for Cooking?
The one you plan to drink is a logical choice, or perhaps a less expensive wine of the same type as the one you're serving. Jug wine is perfectly suitable for cooking and everyday drinking. However, cooking wines usually have salt added, which makes the wine unsuitable for drinking and requires recipe adjustments.

Leftover Wine Is Never a Problem.
With this book you'll find a use for every drop! Pour the leftover wine into a smaller container so that there's less contact with air, close tightly and store in a cool place for a few days. If the wine is to be used for cooking only, you can pour a few drops of olive oil over the surface for additional protection from oxidation. Although sparkling wines lose their spark, they're still useful for cooking.

Which Wine to Drink?
The standard formula of white wine to complement lighter meats (poultry, veal, seafood), red wines with darker meats (beef, game, lamb) and rosé with anything is a good one, based on generations of opinion by wine drinkers. But you'll find many exceptions to this. The kind of wine used in a recipe makes a good companion for drinking. Many think dry champagne is perfect with anything; others think it should be reserved for launching ships.

VERDI
ESTATE BOTTLED

1974
CALIFORNIA
BURGUNDY

PRODUCED AND BOTTLED BY VERDI WINERY
NAPA VALLEY, CALIFORNIA
ALCOHOL 12% BY VOLUME

Brand or vineyard name

Indication of high quality

Vintage year

Generic or varietal name

Source of grapes or wine
and name of bottler

Location of winery

How to Read a Wine Label.

Labels tell a lot, particularly about American wines. The wines we're most concerned with are either generic or varietal. A generic name is a general family group, such as Chablis, Burgundy, Rhine or Chianti. With these, there is no legal requirement to use a specific grape, and several types of grapes are blended to make a wine similar to wines of a European district or type. Because the individual taste of the winemaker is involved, there is a wide variation among generic wines of the same name. Varietals are named for a specific grape, such as Zinfandel, Pinot Chardonnay or Cabernet Sauvignon. By law, if a bottle has a varietal name, at least 51% of the wine must be made from the named grape. Sometimes 100% of the grape has been used, and the label will say so. Here are a few other things to look for on the label:

"Estate Bottled" means that all the grape named came from the vineyard and the wine was processed there. Indication of high quality.

A vintage year guarantees that all the grapes were harvested that year and at least 95% of them are of the type named. Since the quality of the grapes varies from year to year, it's an important point to note.

"Produced by" means that the vineyard processed, fermented and matured at least 75% of the grapes, while "Made by" indicates that most of the wine was probably obtained from independent growers and then bottled by the vineyard.

A location used in the name, such as "Napa Valley Sauterne," shows that at least 75% of the grapes came from that place.

About European labels, we could write a book. Briefly, the more specific the label—the more information on it about the maker, the grape and the location—the more assured you can be that it is a good wine.

The American wine and distilled spirits industry has converted to metric measurements. The differences are small, and the changeover brings American wines into packaging conformity with wines of other countries.

Metric Wine Bottle Sizes

Metric Standards	Approximate Measure Current Cups
375 milliliters	1½ cups
750 milliliters	3 cups
1 liter	4 cups
1.5 liters	6 cups

If the metric measurement does not appear on the label, you will find it on the bottle itself. In some cases, it will be on both.

A Few Serving Tips to Remember.

Wine can be served chilled or unchilled depending on the wine, the weather or your preferences. In general, reds are best at 60 to 65°, slightly cooler than room temperature. Whites and rosés should be at their best around 40 to 50°. Champagne should be thoroughly chilled, but never below 35° or it might be damaged.

Open red wine and leave it uncorked for about an hour before it's served. Even with a jug wine, this airing improves the wine.

Eight-ounce tulip-shaped glasses are fine for all wines, even champagne. Fill half-full so there's plenty of room for the wine's aroma. A regular-sized wine bottle will go once around the table at a dinner for eight people.

Wine Chart

	DRY	MEDIUM	SWEET
RED	Barbera Baco Noir Bordeaux Burgundy Cabernet Sauvignon Chianti Claret Côtes du Rhône Reds Gamay Gamay Beaujolais Grignolino Grignolino Rosé Pinot Noir Pinot St. George Rioja Reds Zinfandel Zinfandel Rosé	Catawba Red Concord Grenache Rosé Lake Country Red Lambrusco Medium-Dry Sherry Rosé d'Anjou Vino Rosso	Aleatico Kosher Concord Malaga Port (Ruby, Tawny, Tinta) Red Malvasia Sweet (Red) Vermouth.
WHITE	Chablis Chenin Blanc Dry Rhine Wine Dry Sauterne Dry Semillon Dry Sherry Dry (White) Vermouth Green Hungarian Grey Riesling Johannisberg Riesling Muscadet Pinot Blanc Pinot Chardonnay Soave Sylvaner Riesling White Burgundy White Chianti	Gewürztraminer Lake Country White Liebfraumilch Orvieto Rhine Wine Riesling Vouvray White Anjou	Angelica Barsac Cream Sherry Haut (Sweet) Sauterne Malvasia Bianca Marsala Muscat de Frontignan Muscatel Sauternes Sweet Semillon Tokay White Kosher Wines

COOKING WITH
Red Wine

Red Wine Main Dishes

Spaghetti with Meatballs

¼ cup olive oil
½ cup finely chopped onion
2 cloves garlic, finely chopped
3 cans (8 ounces each) tomato sauce
1 can (4 ounces) mushroom stems and pieces
½ cup finely chopped green pepper
¼ cup snipped parsley
1 teaspoon salt
½ teaspoon ground pepper
¼ teaspoon sugar
⅛ teaspoon dried basil leaves
⅛ teaspoon ground oregano
1 cup dry red wine
  Meatballs (right)
1 package (16 ounces) spaghetti
  Grated Parmesan cheese

Heat oil in Dutch oven. Cook and stir onion and garlic in hot oil until onion is tender. Stir in tomato sauce, mushrooms (with liquid), green pepper, parsley, salt, pepper, sugar, basil and oregano. Heat to boiling; reduce heat. Cover and simmer, stirring occasionally, 1 hour.

Gradually stir in wine. Cover and simmer, stirring occasionally, 30 minutes. Uncover and simmer, stirring occasionally, 30 minutes longer.

While sauce is simmering, prepare Meatballs. While meatballs are cooking, cook spaghetti as directed on package; drain but do not rinse. Spoon meatballs onto spaghetti; cover with sauce. Serve with cheese.

6 servings.

Meatballs

1½ pounds ground beef
¾ cup dry bread crumbs
½ cup finely chopped onion
¼ cup milk
¼ cup dry red wine
1 egg
1 tablespoon snipped parsley
1½ teaspoons salt
1 teaspoon Worcestershire sauce
⅛ teaspoon ground pepper
¼ cup vegetable oil

Mix all ingredients except oil. Shape by rounded tablespoonfuls into balls. Heat oil in 10-inch skillet. Cook meatballs in hot oil until done, about 20 minutes.

Spaghetti with Meat Sauce

¼ cup olive oil
1½ pounds ground beef
½ cup finely chopped onion
2 cloves garlic, finely chopped
3 cans (8 ounces each) tomato sauce
1 can (4 ounces) mushroom stems and
   pieces
½ cup finely chopped green pepper
¼ cup snipped parsley
2½ teaspoons salt
½ teaspoon ground pepper
¼ teaspoon sugar
⅛ teaspoon dried basil leaves
⅛ teaspoon ground oregano
1 cup dry red wine
1 package (16 ounces) spaghetti
   Grated Parmesan cheese

Heat oil in Dutch oven. Cook and stir beef, onion and garlic in hot oil until beef is light brown; drain off fat. Stir in tomato sauce, mushrooms (with liquid), green pepper, parsley, salt, pepper, sugar, basil and oregano. Heat to boiling; reduce heat. Cover and simmer, stirring occasionally, 1 hour.

Stir in wine. Cover and simmer, stirring occasionally, 30 minutes. Uncover and simmer, stirring occasionally, 30 minutes longer. While sauce is simmering, cook spaghetti as directed on package; drain but do not rinse. Pour meat sauce over hot spaghetti. Serve with cheese.

6 servings.

Chili

1 cup finely chopped onion
1 cup finely chopped green pepper
2 cloves garlic, finely chopped
1 cup dry red wine
¼ cup Worcestershire sauce
2 pounds ground beef
1 tablespoon chili powder
1 teaspoon celery seed
1 teaspoon ground pepper
½ teaspoon salt
½ teaspoon ground cumin
2 cans (16 ounces each) peeled tomatoes
3 cans (15½ ounces each) kidney beans

Cook and stir onion, green pepper and garlic in Dutch oven over low heat 3 minutes. Stir in wine and Worcestershire sauce. Heat to boiling; reduce heat. Simmer uncovered, stirring occasionally, 10 minutes.

While onion mixture is simmering, cook and stir beef until brown; drain off fat.

Stir chili powder, celery seed, pepper, salt and cumin into onion mixture. Simmer uncovered, stirring occasionally, 10 minutes. Stir in tomatoes and beef; break up tomatoes with fork. Heat to boiling; reduce heat. Cover and simmer, stirring occasionally, 30 minutes.

Stir in kidney beans (with liquid). Heat to boiling; reduce heat. Cover and simmer 30 minutes. Uncover and simmer, stirring occasionally, 30 minutes longer.

8 servings.

Beef Loaf

1½ pounds ground beef
3 slices white bread, torn into small pieces
½ cup milk
½ cup sweet red wine
1 egg, beaten
¼ cup finely chopped onion
¼ cup finely chopped celery
¼ cup catsup
1 tablespoon Worcestershire sauce
2 teaspoons salt
¼ teaspoon ground pepper

Heat oven to 350°. Mix all ingredients. Spread in ungreased loaf pan, 8½x4½x2½ inches. Bake 1½ hours.

6 servings.

Beefy Zucchini-Tomato Casserole

3 tablespoons olive or vegetable oil
1½ pounds ground beef
1 medium onion, thinly sliced
3 cans (8 ounces each) tomato sauce
1 cup dry red wine
1 tablespoon sugar
1 teaspoon salt
¼ teaspoon ground pepper
¼ teaspoon ground marjoram
¼ teaspoon dried thyme leaves
⅛ teaspoon dried sweet basil leaves
⅛ teaspoon ground oregano
2 pounds zucchini (about 8 small)
Grated Parmesan cheese

Heat oil in Dutch oven. Cook and stir beef and onion in hot oil until beef is light brown; drain off fat. Stir in remaining ingredients except zucchini and cheese. Heat to boiling; reduce heat. Cover and simmer, stirring occasionally, 1 hour.

Heat oven to 350°. Trim ends from zucchini; cut zucchini lengthwise in half. Place cut sides up in greased baking dish, 13x9x2 inches. Pour on tomato sauce. Bake uncovered 45 minutes. Serve with cheese.

6 servings.

Beef Stroganoff

1 beef bouillon cube
½ cup boiling water
1 pound beef tenderloin, boneless top loin or sirloin steak, about ½ inch thick
2 tablespoons butter or margarine
8 ounces fresh mushrooms, sliced
1 medium onion, thinly sliced
1 small clove garlic, finely chopped
¾ cup dry red wine
½ teaspoon Worcestershire sauce
1 teaspoon salt
3 tablespoons flour
1 cup dairy sour cream
1 package (8 ounces) egg noodles, cooked and drained (4 to 5 cups)

Dissolve bouillon cube in boiling water; cool.

Cut steak across grain into ½-inch strips about 1½ inches long. Melt butter in 10-inch skillet. Cook and stir mushrooms, onion and garlic in butter until onion is tender; remove vegetables.

Cook steak in same skillet until light brown. Stir in wine, Worcestershire sauce and salt. Heat to boiling; reduce heat. Cover and simmer 15 minutes.

Stir bouillon into flour; stir into steak mixture. Add mushroom mixture. Heat to boiling, stirring constantly. Boil and stir 1 minute; reduce heat. Stir in sour cream and heat through. Serve over hot noodles.

4 servings.

Red Wine Beef Stew

Boeuf Bourguignon

2 pounds beef boneless chuck eye roast,* cut into 1-inch cubes
¼ cup all-purpose flour
2 tablespoons olive or vegetable oil
1 clove garlic
1¼ cups red Burgundy or other dry red wine
 About 1½ cups water
½ small bay leaf
1¼ teaspoons salt
2 sprigs parsley
3 slices bacon, diced
18 small white onions
3 tablespoons tomato paste
½ teaspoon dried thyme leaves
⅛ to ¼ teaspoon ground pepper
2 tablespoons butter or margarine
18 small fresh mushroom caps

Heat oven to 325°. Coat beef cubes with flour. Heat oil in Dutch oven. Brown beef cubes in hot oil. Add garlic; cook 1 minute. Remove garlic and fat. Add wine and enough water to just cover the meat. Stir in bay leaf, salt and parsley. Cover and bake 2 hours.

Fry bacon just until limp. Add onions; cook until light brown. Stir bacon and onions into beef cube mixture. Cover and bake until beef cubes are tender, about 40 minutes.

Stir in tomato paste, thyme and pepper. Cover and bake 10 minutes. Melt butter in 6-inch skillet. Cook and stir mushrooms in butter until tender; arrange on top.

4 or 5 servings.

*Beef rolled rump or bottom round roast can be substituted.

Pot roasts can be as different as night and day with just a change of seasonings. The following three recipes offer a delicious choice. Fruited Beef with Wine features the surprising combination of apricots, mushrooms, black olives and ginger. Thyme, lemon juice and sour cream enhance the superb Company Pot Roast gravy. Marinated Pot Roast, Germany's famed *sauerbraten*, calls for the traditional juniper berries, wine and vinegar in the marinade and gingersnaps in the gravy.

Fruited Beef with Wine

1 cup water
1 cup dried apricots,* cut into halves
2 teaspoons salt
½ teaspoon ground ginger
¼ teaspoon ground pepper
4- to 5-pound beef shoulder pot roast
1 tablespoon shortening
1½ cups chopped onion
2 cloves garlic, finely chopped
½ cup dry red wine
1 can (6 ounces) pitted ripe olives, drained
5 ounces mushrooms, sliced (about 2 cups)

Pour water over apricots; reserve. Mix salt, ginger and pepper; rub over beef roast. Heat shortening in skillet or Dutch oven until melted; brown beef on all sides. Drain off fat; add onion, garlic and wine. Heat to boiling; reduce heat. Cover tightly and simmer on top of range or in 325° oven 2 hours.

Add apricots, olives and mushrooms. Cover and cook until beef is tender, about 1 hour. (Pictured on cover.)

12 to 16 servings.

*1 cup pitted prunes (about ½ pound) can be substituted.

Company Pot Roast

3 tablespoons vegetable oil
3- to 4-pound beef rolled rump roast*
¾ cup dry red wine
2 cloves garlic, finely chopped
2 medium carrots, cut into julienne strips
2 medium onions, thinly sliced and separated into rings
¾ cup dairy sour cream
1½ teaspoons salt
1 teaspoon ground pepper
½ teaspoon dried thyme leaves
½ cup water
2 tablespoons flour
2 tablespoons lemon juice

Heat oven to 325°. Heat oil in Dutch oven. Brown roast in hot oil; remove roast. Mix wine, garlic, carrots, onions, sour cream, salt, pepper and thyme in Dutch oven.

Return roast to Dutch oven. Cover and bake until roast is tender, about 3½ hours, turning 2 or 3 times during baking. Remove roast and vegetables to heated platter; keep warm while preparing gravy.

Skim fat off liquid. Shake water and flour in covered jar. Stir flour mixture slowly into liquid. Heat to boiling, stirring constantly. Boil and stir 1 minute. Stir in lemon juice; cook 1 minute. Slice roast thinly; serve with gravy. (Pictured on page 18.)

About 10 servings.

*Beef bottom round or boneless chuck eye roast can be substituted.

Marinated Pot Roast

Sauerbraten

- 1 cup dry red wine
- ½ cup red wine vinegar
- 1½ cups cold water
- 1 large onion, thinly sliced
- 5 black peppercorns, crushed
- 4 whole juniper berries, crushed
- 1 large bay leaf
- 3- to 4-pound beef rolled rump roast
- 3 tablespoons shortening
- ½ cup water
- ½ cup gingersnap crumbs
  Potato Dumplings (right)

Mix wine, vinegar, 1½ cups water, the onion, peppercorns, juniper berries and bay leaf. Heat to boiling. Remove from heat; cool in refrigerator to room temperature.

Pierce surface of roast with fork. Place roast in 3-quart glass bowl; pour on marinade. Cover tightly and refrigerate 2 to 3 days, turning roast several times each day.

Remove roast from marinade and pat dry. Strain marinade, reserving liquid and discarding onion and spices. Melt shortening in Dutch oven. Brown roast in shortening 10 minutes. Remove roast; pour off fat.

Heat 2 cups of the reserved marinade and ½ cup water to boiling in Dutch oven (reserve remaining marinade). Return roast to Dutch oven; reduce heat. Cover and simmer until roast is tender, about 2 hours.

Remove roast to heated platter; cover with aluminum foil to keep warm. Measure liquid in Dutch oven into large measuring cup; skim off fat. Add enough reserved marinade to measure 2½ cups if necessary. (If liquid measures more than 2½ cups, boil rapidly to reduce amount to 2½ cups.) Heat liquid and gingersnap crumbs over medium heat, stirring frequently, 10 minutes;

strain. Serve gravy with roast and Potato Dumplings.

6 to 8 servings.

Potato Dumplings

- 2 slices white bread, crusts removed
- 2 tablespoons butter or margarine
- ½ cup all-purpose flour
- ½ cup uncooked regular farina (wheat cereal)
- 1½ teaspoons salt
- ⅛ teaspoon ground nutmeg
- ⅛ teaspoon ground white pepper
- 3½ cups riced cooked potatoes (4 or 5 medium baking potatoes)
- 2 eggs, beaten
- 4 quarts water
- 2 teaspoons salt
- ½ cup dry bread crumbs
- 2 tablespoons butter or margarine

Cut bread into ½-inch cubes. Cook bread cubes in 2 tablespoons butter in 8-inch skillet over medium heat, stirring frequently, until golden brown. Drain on paper towels.

Mix flour, farina, 1½ teaspoons salt, the nutmeg, pepper and potatoes. Stir in eggs; beat until dough holds its shape. Flour hands lightly. Shape about 2 tablespoons dough into ball. Press hole in center with fingertip; drop 4 bread cubes into hole. Seal by shaping into ball again. Repeat with remaining dough and bread cubes.

Heat water and 2 teaspoons salt to boiling in 6-quart kettle. While water heats, cook and stir crumbs in 2 tablespoons butter over low heat until butter is absorbed; reserve.

Drop dumplings into boiling water. Stir once or twice; reduce heat. Simmer uncovered until dumplings rise to top, 12 to 15 minutes. Cook 1 minute. Remove with slotted spoon; sprinkle with bread crumbs.

Red Brisket

3-pound beef corned brisket
1 clove garlic, slivered
½ cup bottled creamy onion salad
   dressing
½ cup sweet red wine
⅓ cup catsup
½ cup water
2 tablespoons flour

Heat oven to 325°. Make about 5 evenly spaced slits about ½ inch deep in brisket; insert garlic sliver into each slit. Place brisket in baking pan, 9x9x2 inches. Pour dressing over brisket; turn brisket. Cover with aluminum foil and bake 1 hour.

Spoon drippings and dressing up over brisket. Mix wine and catsup; pour over brisket. Cover and bake until brisket is tender, about 2 hours. Remove to heated platter; keep warm while preparing gravy.

Skim fat off liquid. Measure 2 cups liquid into 2-quart saucepan. Shake water and flour in covered jar. Stir flour mixture gradually into broth. Heat to boiling, stirring constantly. Boil and stir 1 minute. Thinly slice brisket diagonally across grain; serve with gravy.

8 servings.

Pork Chow Mein

1 pound pork blade or arm steak
1 cup dry red wine
1 cup boiling water
1 cup sliced celery
½ cup finely chopped onion
3 tablespoons soy sauce
2 teaspoons instant beef bouillon
1 teaspoon monosodium glutamate
1 jar (2½ ounces) sliced mushrooms,
   drained (reserve liquid)
   Dry red wine
¼ cup cornstarch
1 can (16 ounces) Chinese vegetables,
   drained
2 tablespoons brown gravy sauce
   (molasses type)
3 cups chow mein noodles

Trim excess fat from steak. Cut steak diagonally into very thin strips. Lightly grease 10-inch skillet with excess fat. Brown steak; drain off fat.

Stir in 1 cup wine, the water, celery, onion, soy sauce, instant bouillon and monosodium glutamate. Heat to boiling; reduce heat. Cover and simmer 30 minutes.

Measure reserved mushroom liquid; add enough wine to measure ¼ cup if necessary. Stir liquid into cornstarch; stir gradually into steak mixture. Stir in mushrooms, Chinese vegetables and gravy sauce. Heat to boiling. Boil and stir 1 minute. Serve over chow mein noodles.

4 servings.

White Wine Beef and Vegetable Stew (page 41) and Rock Cornish Hens Bourguignon (page 25).

Preparing an elegant but bountiful welcome for a crowd: Company Pot Roast (page 14).

Summertime specials: Fresh Fruit Soup (page 30) to start; Zucchini Toss (page 32) for salad.

A choice of happy endings: Red Wine Apple Pie (page 38) or Glazed Cherry Tarts (page 37).

Wine-Mushroom Pork Steaks

4 pork blade or arm steaks, ½ inch
   thick (1½ to 2 pounds)
2 teaspoons vegetable oil
1 medium green pepper, cut into rings
1 clove garlic, crushed
8 ounces fresh mushrooms, sliced
½ cup dry red wine
1½ teaspoons salt
¼ teaspoon ground pepper

Brown steaks in 10-inch skillet over low heat. Remove from skillet.

Heat oil in same skillet. Cook and stir green pepper, garlic and mushrooms in hot oil over low heat until mushrooms are tender, about 5 minutes.

Place steaks on green pepper and mushrooms; add wine. Sprinkle steaks with salt and pepper. Heat to boiling; reduce heat. Cover and simmer until steaks are tender, about 40 minutes.

4 servings.

Pork Chop Rosé

4 pork blade, rib or loin chops, ½ to ¾
   inch thick
1 teaspoon salt
1 small onion, thinly sliced
½ cup rosé wine
   Grated peel of 1 large orange
   Juice of 1 large orange
2 tablespoons brown sugar
¼ teaspoon ground allspice
1 small orange, thinly sliced

Brown chops in 10-inch skillet over medium heat; drain off fat. Sprinkle chops with salt; arrange onion slices on chops. Mix wine, orange peel, orange juice, brown sugar and allspice; pour into skillet. Heat to boiling; reduce heat. Cover and simmer 30 minutes. Arrange orange slices on chops. Cover and simmer until chops are tender, about 15 minutes. Serve pan liquid with chops if desired.

2 servings.

Seasoned City Chicken

1 egg
¼ cup water
1 envelope (about .7 ounce)
   blue cheese salad dressing mix
6 city chicken* (about 1½ pounds)
½ to ¾ cup dry bread crumbs
¼ cup shortening
1 teaspoon salt
⅛ teaspoon ground pepper
¼ cup dry red wine

Beat egg and water slightly; stir in salad dressing mix. Dip city chicken into egg mixture; coat with bread crumbs.

Melt shortening in 10-inch skillet. Brown city chicken in hot shortening. Sprinkle with salt and pepper; add wine. Heat to boiling; reduce heat. Cover and simmer until done, about 1 hour. Add additional wine to cover bottom of skillet when necessary.

4 servings.

*Equal parts of pork and veal cubes placed on skewers.

Country Ribs

1 cup sweet red wine
½ cup chili sauce
⅓ cup vinegar
¼ cup honey
2 tablespoons soy sauce
1 tablespoon Worcestershire sauce
2 teaspoons salt
2 teaspoons dry mustard
1 teaspoon horseradish
1 teaspoon red pepper sauce
½ teaspoon ground pepper
½ teaspoon paprika
3 tablespoons vegetable oil
3 pounds pork country-style ribs

Mix all ingredients except oil and ribs in saucepan. Heat to boiling, stirring constantly. Remove from heat.

Heat oven to 350°. Heat oil in Dutch oven over low heat. Brown half of the ribs in hot oil; remove ribs. Repeat with remaining ribs; drain off fat.

Return ribs to Dutch oven; pour sauce over ribs. Cover and bake 1 hour. Uncover and bake until done, about 30 minutes. Remove ribs to serving bowl. Strain sauce; skim off fat. Pour sauce over ribs.

4 servings.

Lasagne

1 pound bulk Italian sausage or ground beef
¾ cup finely chopped onion
1 clove garlic, finely chopped
1 can (16 ounces) tomatoes
1 cup dry red wine
1 can (6 ounces) tomato paste
2 tablespoons sugar
2 tablespoons parsley flakes
1 teaspoon salt
1 teaspoon dried basil leaves
1 package (8 ounces) lasagne noodles, cooked and drained
Cheese Filling (below)
¾ pound mozzarella cheese, shredded
½ cup grated Parmesan cheese

Cook and stir sausage, onion and garlic in Dutch oven until sausage is brown; drain off fat. Add tomatoes; break up with fork. Stir in wine, tomato paste, sugar, parsley flakes, salt and basil. Heat to boiling, stirring occasionally; reduce heat. Simmer uncovered until mixture is consistency of spaghetti sauce, about 45 minutes.

Heat oven to 350°. Reserve ½ cup of the meat sauce for thin top layer. Layer ⅓ each of the noodles, remaining meat sauce, Cheese Filling and mozzarella cheese in ungreased baking pan, 13x9x2 inches. Repeat 2 times. Spread reserved meat sauce over top; sprinkle with Parmesan cheese. Bake uncovered 45 minutes.

8 to 10 servings.

Cheese Filling

Mix 2 cartons (12 ounces each) ricotta or creamed cottage cheese (3 cups), ½ cup grated Parmesan cheese, 1 tablespoon parsley flakes, 1½ teaspoons salt and 1½ teaspoons dried oregano leaves.

Eggplant-Lamb Bake

Moussaka

1 medium eggplant (1½ to 2 pounds)
1 teaspoon salt
½ cup all-purpose flour
   Vegetable oil
2 tablespoons butter or margarine
1 pound ground lamb
½ cup chopped onion
1 can (8 ounces) tomato sauce
1 cup dry red wine
2 tablespoons snipped parsley
½ teaspoon salt
¼ teaspoon ground pepper
¼ teaspoon ground nutmeg
1 egg, beaten
½ cup grated kefalotyri, Parmesan or
   Romano cheese
¼ cup dry bread crumbs
3 tablespoons butter or margarine
3 tablespoons flour
½ teaspoon salt
¼ teaspoon ground nutmeg
1¾ cups milk
2 eggs
¼ cup grated kefalotyri, Parmesan or
   Romano cheese
¼ cup dry bread crumbs
¼ cup grated kefalotyri, Parmesan or
   Romano cheese

Pare eggplant; cut crosswise into ¼-inch slices. Sprinkle slices with 1 teaspoon salt. Coat with ½ cup flour; shake off excess. Heat 2 tablespoons oil. Fry several eggplant slices in hot oil until golden brown. Repeat with remaining slices, adding more oil when necessary; drain on paper towels.

Melt 2 tablespoons butter in 10-inch skillet. Cook and stir lamb and onion in butter over medium heat until lamb is brown. Stir in tomato sauce, wine, parsley, ½ teaspoon salt, the pepper and ¼ teaspoon nutmeg. Cook uncovered until half of the liquid is absorbed, about 20 minutes. Stir in 1 beaten egg, ½ cup cheese and ¼ cup bread crumbs. Remove from heat.

Heat oven to 375°. Melt 3 tablespoons butter in 2-quart saucepan. Stir in 3 tablespoons flour, ½ teaspoon salt and ¼ teaspoon nutmeg. Cook over low heat, stirring constantly, until mixture is smooth and bubbly. Add milk, stirring constantly, until sauce boils. Beat 2 eggs slightly. Stir small amount of hot milk mixture into eggs. Stir egg-milk mixture back into hot mixture in pan. Stir in ¼ cup cheese.

Grease baking dish, 12x7½x2 or 9x9x2 inches. Sprinkle ¼ cup bread crumbs evenly in dish. Arrange half of the eggplant slices in dish; cover with lamb mixture. Sprinkle with 2 tablespoons of the cheese; top with remaining eggplant slices. Pour sauce over eggplant slices; sprinkle with remaining 2 tablespoons cheese. Bake uncovered 45 minutes. Remove from oven; let stand 20 minutes before serving.

6 servings.

Originally a Rumanian specialty, Moussaka is an exotic treat that is popular throughout Greece and the Near East. The intriguing blend of seasonings and the special affinity of eggplant for lamb make an exceptionally delicious casserole.

If you're beginning to experiment with game, this spicy and tender *hasenpfeffer* (pepper hare) is a perfect introduction. Rabbit is becoming more readily available in the frozen food section of the supermarket. Because the taste and texture of rabbit are so delicate, European butchers usually group it with poultry.

Spicy Braised Rabbit

Hasenpfeffer

2½- to 3-pound frozen rabbit, thawed and cut into serving pieces
 ½ teaspoon salt
 ⅓ cup all-purpose flour
 ½ pound bacon, cut into ¼-inch pieces
 ½ cup finely chopped shallots or onion
 1 clove garlic, finely chopped
 1 cup dry red wine
 1 cup water
 1 tablespoon instant chicken bouillon
 1 tablespoon currant jelly
 10 black peppercorns, crushed
 1 small bay leaf
 ¼ teaspoon dried rosemary leaves, crushed
 ⅛ teaspoon dried thyme leaves
 2 teaspoons lemon juice
 3 tablespoons water
 2 tablespoons flour

Sprinkle rabbit with salt. Coat with ⅓ cup flour; shake off excess.

Fry bacon in Dutch oven over medium heat until crisp; remove bacon and drain on paper towels. Brown a few pieces of rabbit in hot bacon fat; remove browned pieces. Repeat with remaining rabbit. Remove all but 2 tablespoons fat.

Cook and stir shallots and garlic in hot fat in Dutch oven until shallots are tender, about 4 minutes. Stir in wine, 1 cup water and the instant bouillon. Heat to boiling. Stir in jelly, peppercorns, bay leaf, rosemary and thyme. Return rabbit and bacon to Dutch oven. Heat to boiling; reduce heat. Cover and simmer until rabbit is tender, about 1½ hours.

Remove bay leaf and discard. Place rabbit on warm platter; keep warm while preparing gravy. Stir lemon juice into liquid in Dutch oven. Shake 3 tablespoons water and 2 tablespoons flour in covered jar. Stir flour mixture slowly into liquid. Heat to boiling, stirring constantly. Boil and stir 1 minute. (If gravy is too thick, stir in more water until of desired consistency.) Serve gravy with rabbit.

4 servings.

Rock Cornish Hens Bourguignon

1 teaspoon salt
¼ teaspoon ground cloves
¼ teaspoon ground nutmeg
¼ teaspoon ground pepper
¼ teaspoon ground thyme
4 frozen Rock Cornish hens (about 1 pound each), thawed
4 slices bacon, cut in half
1¼ cups red Burgundy or other dry red wine
½ teaspoon instant chicken bouillon
½ cup boiling water
2 tablespoons finely chopped onion
2 tablespoons snipped parsley
3 to 4 cups cooked brown or white rice
⅓ cup currant jelly

Heat oven to 350°. Mix salt, cloves, nutmeg, pepper and thyme; rub outsides and cavities of hens with seasoning mixture. Place hens breast sides up on rack in shallow roasting pan. Crisscross bacon slices over hens. Mix wine, instant bouillon, water, onion and parsley; pour into roasting pan.

Roast uncovered 1 hour. Increase oven temperature to 400°. Roast until drumstick meat feels very soft when pressed, about 10 minutes.

Remove hens to warm platter. Remove bacon and cut into small pieces. Stir bacon into rice. Strain hot juices from roasting pan into saucepan; stir in currant jelly. Heat, stirring constantly, until jelly is melted; skim off fat. Arrange rice around hens on platter; spoon sauce over hens. (Pictured on page 17.)

4 servings.

Fruited Chicken

2 tablespoons butter or margarine
2 tablespoons vegetable oil
2½- to 3-pound broiler-fryer chicken, cut up
½ cup dry red wine
2 teaspoons instant chicken bouillon
1 can (21 ounces) cherry pie filling
1 can (13¼ ounces) pineapple tidbits, drained
1 jar (2½ ounces) whole mushrooms, drained

Heat oven to 350°. Measure butter and oil into baking dish, 13x9x2 inches. Heat in oven until butter is melted. Place chicken pieces skin sides up in baking dish. Bake uncovered 1 hour; drain off fat.

Heat wine and instant bouillon to boiling in 2-quart saucepan. Boil 1 minute. Remove from heat. Stir in remaining ingredients; spoon over chicken. Cover and bake until bubbly, about 20 minutes.

4 servings.

Chicken in Wine

Coq au Vin

- 6 slices bacon
- 3- to 3½-pound broiler-fryer chicken, cut up
- 6 small onions
- 8 ounces fresh mushrooms, sliced
- 4 potatoes, quartered
- 1 teaspoon instant chicken bouillon
- 1 cup boiling water
- 1 cup red Burgundy or other dry red wine
- 1 clove garlic, crushed
- 1 teaspoon salt
  Bouquet garni*
- 3 tablespoons water
- 2 tablespoons flour
  Snipped parsley

Fry bacon until crisp; remove bacon and drain on paper towels. Brown chicken in hot bacon fat, about 20 minutes.

Push chicken to one side. Add onions and mushrooms. Cook and stir until mushrooms are tender; drain off fat. Mix chicken, onions and mushrooms.

Crumble bacon into skillet. Stir in potatoes, instant bouillon, boiling water, wine, garlic, salt and bouquet garni. Heat to boiling; reduce heat. Cover and simmer until chicken is done, about 1 hour.

Remove bouquet garni and discard. Remove chicken and vegetables to warm serving dish; keep warm while preparing gravy. Skim excess fat off liquid. Shake 3 tablespoons water and the flour in covered jar. Stir flour mixture slowly into liquid. Heat to boiling, stirring constantly. Boil and stir 1 minute. Pour sauce over chicken; sprinkle with parsley.

4 servings.

*Tie 2 large sprigs parsley, 1 bay leaf and ½ teaspoon dried thyme leaves in cheesecloth bag.

Salmon Steak Bake

2 packages (12 ounces each) frozen
  salmon steaks
1 teaspoon salt
⅛ teaspoon ground pepper
1 tablespoon butter or margarine,
  melted
½ cup dry red wine
¼ cup finely chopped onion
2 tablespoons lemon juice
1 tablespoon cold water
½ teaspoon cornstarch
½ cup seedless green grapes (optional)

Heat oven to 475°. Place frozen salmon steaks in buttered baking dish, 12x7½x2 inches. Sprinkle with salt and pepper; brush with melted butter. Bake uncovered 15 minutes.

While steaks are baking, heat wine, onion and lemon juice to boiling in 1½-quart saucepan; reduce heat. Simmer uncovered 5 minutes. Stir water into cornstarch; stir into wine sauce. Heat to boiling. Boil and stir 1 minute. Stir in grapes. Spoon sauce over salmon. Bake uncovered 5 minutes. (Pictured on page 53.)

4 servings.

Tuna Tetrazzini

¼ cup butter or margarine
¼ cup all-purpose flour
½ teaspoon salt
¼ teaspoon ground pepper
1 cup whipping cream
¾ cup water
¼ cup dry red wine
1 teaspoon instant chicken bouillon
2 cans (6½ ounces each) tuna, drained
1 package (7 ounces) thin spaghetti,
  cooked and drained
1 jar (2½ ounces) sliced mushrooms,
  drained
1 jar (2 ounces) pimiento, drained and
  chopped
½ cup grated Parmesan cheese

Heat oven to 350°. Melt butter in 10-inch skillet over low heat. Stir in flour, salt and pepper. Cook over low heat, stirring constantly, until mixture is smooth and bubbly. Remove from heat.

Stir in cream, water, wine and instant bouillon. Heat to boiling, stirring constantly. Boil and stir 1 minute. Stir in tuna, spaghetti, mushrooms and pimiento. Pour into ungreased 2-quart casserole. Sprinkle with cheese. Bake uncovered until bubbly, about 30 minutes. Place under broiler just long enough to brown.

6 servings.

Tangy Tomato Fish

2 tablespoons vegetable oil
½ cup finely chopped onion
2 cloves garlic, crushed
¼ cup snipped parsley
1 teaspoon salt
4 drops red pepper sauce
½ cup dry red wine
1 can (6 ounces) tomato paste
2 packages (16 ounces each) frozen
   haddock fillets, partially thawed
   and cut into 1-inch cubes

Heat oven to 350°. Heat oil in 8-inch skillet. Cook and stir onion and garlic in hot oil until onion is tender, about 4 minutes; drain off oil. Stir in parsley, salt and pepper sauce. Mix wine and tomato paste; stir into onion mixture.

Place haddock cubes in ungreased baking dish, 12x7½x2 inches; spoon sauce over haddock, spreading evenly. Cover and bake until haddock flakes easily, about 30 minutes. (Pictured on page 53.)

6 servings.

Continental Eggs

1 tablespoon butter or margarine
6 small onions, quartered
1 package (4½ ounces) sliced cooked
   ham, cut into ¼-inch strips
1 jar (2½ ounces) sliced mushrooms,
   drained
2 tablespoons flour
1 clove garlic, crushed
½ teaspoon sugar
¼ teaspoon salt
⅛ teaspoon ground thyme
⅛ teaspoon ground marjoram
   Dash of ground pepper
1 cup dry red wine
½ cup water
1 teaspoon instant beef bouillon
4 hard-cooked eggs, cut
   lengthwise into 4 slices
4 slices buttered toast

Melt butter in 10-inch skillet. Cook and stir onions in butter until onions are light brown. Add ham and mushrooms; cook and stir over low heat 2 minutes.

Stir in flour, garlic, sugar, salt, thyme, marjoram and pepper. Cook over low heat, stirring constantly, until hot and bubbly. Remove from heat.

Stir in wine, water and instant bouillon. Heat to boiling, stirring constantly; reduce heat. Cover and simmer 20 minutes. Arrange egg slices on toast; spoon sauce over egg slices.

4 servings.

Red Wine Side Dishes

Wine Meatballs

- 1 pound ground beef
- 3 tablespoons dry red wine
- 1½ teaspoons bleu cheese garni
- 1 teaspoon salt
- 1 cup dry red wine
- 1 cup water
- 2 teaspoons instant beef bouillon

Mix beef, 3 tablespoons wine and the bleu cheese garni. Shape into 1-inch balls. Refrigerate 15 minutes to 1 hour.

Heat meatballs and remaining ingredients to boiling; reduce heat. Simmer uncovered until meatballs are done, about 2½ minutes. Transfer meatballs to chafing dish. Skim fat off liquid; pour liquid into chafing dish to 1-inch depth (about 1 cup).

8 appetizer servings.

Cream Cheese—Deviled Ham Dip

- 1 package (8 ounces) cream cheese, softened
- 1 can (4½ ounces) deviled ham
- ¼ cup dry red wine
- 3 tablespoons finely chopped dill pickle
- 1 teaspoon instant minced onion
- 1 teaspoon Worcestershire sauce
- ¼ teaspoon instant minced garlic
- ¼ teaspoon dry mustard

Beat cream cheese, deviled ham and wine in small mixer bowl until creamy. Stir in remaining ingredients. Serve immediately as a dip or refrigerate to serve as a spread.

1⅔ cups.

Summer Fruit Bowl

3 medium bananas
4 medium oranges, pared and sectioned
   (about 3 cups)
1 cup strawberries, halved
1 cup seedless green grapes, halved
½ cup dairy sour cream
2 tablespoons sweet red wine
1 tablespoon honey

Slice bananas into bowl. Cover completely with remaining fruit; cover bowl and refrigerate.

Just before serving, mix remaining ingredients; pour over fruit. Toss until fruit is coated.

10 servings.

Fresh Fruit Soup

3 tablespoons sugar
3 tablespoons cornstarch
⅛ teaspoon salt
1 cup water
1¼ cups rosé wine
1½ cups cranberry juice
3 cups fresh fruit, such as strawberries,
   blueberries, bananas, seedless green
   grapes, cantaloupe, cherries

Mix sugar, cornstarch and salt in 3-quart saucepan; stir in water and wine. Heat to boiling, stirring constantly. Boil and stir 1 minute. Remove from heat. Stir in cranberry juice. Cover loosely and refrigerate until chilled.

Stir in fruit. Serve with sour cream or whipped cream if desired. (Pictured on page 19.)

6 servings.

Beets in Red Wine Sauce

2 tablespoons butter or margarine
1 tablespoon cornstarch
1 tablespoon brown sugar
¼ teaspoon salt
   Dash of ground cloves
1 can (16 ounces) cut beets, drained
   (reserve ¼ cup liquid)
½ cup dry red wine

Melt butter in 8-inch skillet over low heat. Mix cornstarch, brown sugar, salt and cloves; stir into melted butter. Stir in reserved beet liquid and wine. Heat to boiling, stirring constantly. Boil and stir 1 minute. Stir in beets; heat through.

4 servings.

Saucy Red Cabbage

Rotkohl

2 tablespoons butter or margarine
1 apple, pared and sliced
1 onion, thinly sliced
½ head red cabbage, coarsely shredded
½ cup dry red wine
¼ cup red wine vinegar
¼ cup apple jelly
2 whole cloves
1 tablespoon cornstarch

Melt butter in Dutch oven over medium heat. Cook and stir apple and onion in butter until apple is soft but not mushy. Stir in cabbage, wine, vinegar, jelly and cloves. Heat to boiling; reduce heat. Cover and simmer until cabbage is tender, about 30 minutes; drain, reserving liquid.

Mix 2 tablespoons reserved liquid into cornstarch. Stir in remaining liquid gradually; stir until smooth. Return to Dutch oven. Heat to boiling, stirring constantly. Boil and stir 1 minute. Pour over cabbage.

6 or 7 servings.

Red Cabbage in Red Wine

Chou Rouge au Vin Rouge

4 ounces salt pork, diced
½ cup chopped onion
2 tablespoons flour
½ cup dry red wine
1 medium head red cabbage, coarsely
   shredded (about 12 cups)
⅛ teaspoon ground pepper

Heat oven to 350°. Cook and stir salt pork in Dutch oven over medium heat until crisp; add onion. Cook and stir until onion is tender. Stir in flour. Remove from heat. Stir in remaining ingredients. Cover and bake until cabbage is tender, about 1 hour. Season with salt if desired.

6 or 7 servings.

Scalloped Corn Deluxe

4 ears fresh corn*
1 tablespoon sugar
1 tablespoon lemon juice
1 gallon cold water
2 tablespoons butter or margarine
¼ cup finely chopped onion
¼ cup finely chopped green pepper
2 tablespoons flour
1 teaspoon salt
½ teaspoon paprika
¼ teaspoon dry mustard
   Dash of ground pepper
½ cup rosé wine
¼ cup milk
½ cup shredded natural Cheddar cheese
1 egg, slightly beaten
1 tablespoon butter or margarine
⅓ cup cracker crumbs

Heat corn, sugar, lemon juice and water to boiling in Dutch oven or large kettle. Boil uncovered 2 minutes. Remove from heat; let stand 10 minutes. Cut enough kernels from ears to measure 2 cups.

Heat oven to 350°. Melt 2 tablespoons butter in 8-inch skillet. Cook and stir onion and green pepper in butter until onion is tender. Remove from heat. Stir in flour, salt, paprika, mustard and pepper. Cook over low heat, stirring constantly, until mixture is hot and bubbly. Remove from heat.

Gradually stir wine and milk into flour mixture. Heat to boiling, stirring constantly. Boil and stir 1 minute. Stir in cheese, egg and corn kernels. Pour into ungreased 1-quart casserole.

Melt 1 tablespoon butter. Remove from heat. Stir in cracker crumbs. Sprinkle crumbs evenly over corn mixture. Bake uncovered until bubbly, 30 to 35 minutes.

4 servings.

*1 package (10 ounces) frozen whole kernel corn, cooked and drained, or 1 can (16 ounces) whole kernel corn, drained, can be used. Omit sugar, lemon juice and water.

Ever since the pilgrims harvested their first crop, corn has been a great American food. With rosé wine, cheese and green pepper, it attains an elegance and zest never dreamed of by those at Plymouth Rock! At a backyard barbecue—or at Thanksgiving dinner—our version will add an original touch to the traditional favorite.

Blue Cheese-Red Wine Dressing

⅓ cup crumbled blue or Roquefort cheese
⅔ cup vegetable oil
3 tablespoons dry red wine
2 tablespoons wine vinegar
½ teaspoon salt
½ teaspoon paprika
¼ teaspoon dry mustard
⅛ teaspoon ground pepper
Dash of garlic powder
Salad greens

Mash cheese with fork. Mix remaining ingredients except salad greens; stir gradually into cheese. Serve over salad greens.

About 1 cup.

Zucchini Toss

¼ cup vegetable oil, olive oil or combination of both
2 tablespoons dry red wine
1 tablespoon red wine vinegar
½ teaspoon salt
¼ teaspoon dry mustard
¼ teaspoon paprika
½ head lettuce
½ small bunch romaine
1 medium zucchini, thinly sliced
½ cup sliced radishes
2 green onions, sliced
2 tablespoons crumbled blue cheese (optional)

Shake oil, wine, vinegar, salt, mustard and paprika in tightly covered jar. Refrigerate until chilled.

Tear greens into bite-size pieces in large salad bowl. Mix in remaining ingredients. Shake dressing; pour over salad. Toss until greens glisten. (Pictured on page 19.)

3 or 4 servings.

Cranberry-Orange Salad Mold

1 package (3 ounces) lemon-flavored
  gelatin
1 envelope unflavored gelatin
¾ cup boiling water
½ cup dry red wine
1 orange
1 can (16 ounces) whole cranberry sauce
  Salad greens
  Mayonnaise or salad dressing

Mix gelatins. Pour boiling water on gelatin; stir until dissolved. Stir in wine. Grate peel of orange. Pare and section orange. Cut up orange sections; place in blender with grated peel. Cover and puree. Stir orange puree into gelatin mixture; cool slightly.

Break up cranberry sauce with fork; stir into gelatin mixture. Pour into six ⅔-cup molds. Refrigerate until firm, at least 4 hours. Unmold onto salad greens; serve with mayonnaise.

6 servings.

Curried Apples

2 apples, cored and cut into ¼-inch
  rings
⅔ cup dry red wine
¼ cup butter or margarine, melted
¼ cup brown sugar (packed)
¼ teaspoon curry powder

Soak apple rings in wine in covered shallow bowl or baking dish 3 hours, stirring occasionally; drain.

Set oven control to broil and/or 550°. Place apple rings on rack in broiler pan. Broil rings 5 inches from heat 3 minutes; turn.

Mix remaining ingredients; spoon over rings. Broil until glazed and light brown, about 1½ minutes.

4 servings.

Hot Wine Jelly

1 tablespoon crushed dried hot peppers
2 cups sweet red wine
3 cups sugar
1 teaspoon yellow food color
¾ teaspoon red food color
½ bottle (6-ounce size) liquid pectin

Stir peppers into wine. Cover and let stand at least 3 hours. While peppers are marinating, prepare jars (see note).

Strain wine into 3-quart saucepan; stir in sugar and food colors. Heat over low heat, stirring constantly, until sugar is dissolved, about 5 minutes. Remove from heat. Immediately stir in pectin; skim off foam. Fill jars and seal with paraffin. Serve as an accompaniment to meats.

Four or five 8-ounce jars.

Note: To prepare jars, place clean jelly jars in pan with folded cloth on bottom. Cover with hot (not boiling) water and heat to boiling. Boil gently 15 minutes; keep jars in hot water until ready to use. When ready to fill, remove jars from water and drain.

Red Wine Desserts

Pears Poached in Red Wine

Poires au Vin Rouge

   6 small pears, pared, cored and halved
      Juice of 1 lemon
   2 cups dry red wine
1⅓ cups sugar
   2-inch cinnamon stick

Dip pears into lemon juice. Heat wine, sugar and cinnamon stick in 10-inch skillet, stirring constantly, until sugar is dissolved and mixture boils; reduce heat and add pears. Simmer uncovered until pears are soft but not mushy when pierced with sharp knife, about 15 minutes.

Cool pears in syrup until lukewarm; discard cinnamon stick. Remove pears to dessert dishes with slotted spoon. Spoon syrup over pears. Serve warm or refrigerate until cool.

6 servings.

Spicy Wine Fruit

   2-inch cinnamon stick
   6 whole cloves
 ½ cup water
 ½ cup sweet red wine
 ¼ cup sugar
   2 tablespoons lemon juice
   1 package (11 ounces) mixed dried fruit
   2 bananas

Tie cinnamon stick and cloves in cheesecloth bag. Heat cheesecloth bag, water, wine, sugar and lemon juice to boiling in 2-quart saucepan. Stir in dried fruit. Heat to boiling; reduce heat. Simmer uncovered, stirring occasionally, until fruit is plump and tender, 10 to 15 minutes. Refrigerate uncovered, stirring occasionally, at least 3 hours but no longer than 24 hours.

Remove cheesecloth bag. Slice bananas and stir into fruit mixture until coated with syrup. Drain fruit, reserving syrup. Serve fruit with some of the reserved syrup.

5 or 6 servings.

Creamy Cheesecake

1¼ cups graham cracker crumbs (about
    16 square crackers)
2 tablespoons sugar
¼ cup butter or margarine, melted
2 packages (8 ounces each) cream
    cheese, softened
2 eggs
¾ cup sugar
1 tablespoon sweet red wine
    Almond Topping (right)
    Slivered almonds
    Candied cherry halves

Heat oven to 350°. Mix cracker crumbs and 2 tablespoons sugar; stir in melted butter. Press crumb mixture firmly and evenly against bottom and side of 9-inch pie plate.

Beat cream cheese slightly in small mixer bowl. Add eggs, ¾ cup sugar and 1 tablespoon wine; beat until light and fluffy. Pour into crumb crust. Bake until firm, 25 minutes. Cool 5 minutes.

Drop Almond Topping by teaspoonfuls onto cheesecake. Spread gently over cake; cool. Refrigerate at least 3 hours. Garnish with slivered almonds and candied cherry halves.

Almond Topping

2 cups ground almonds (about two
    4-ounce packages slivered almonds)
½ cup sugar
⅓ cup sweet red wine
1 tablespoon grated orange peel

Mix ground almonds and sugar. Stir in wine and orange peel.

Chocolate-Wine Balls

    1 package (6 ounces) semisweet
        chocolate chips
    ¼ cup honey
    2½ cups finely crushed vanilla wafers
        (about 55)
    2 cups ground walnuts
    ⅓ cup sweet red wine
        Granulated sugar

Heat chocolate chips and honey in 3-quart saucepan over low heat, stirring constantly, until chocolate is melted. Remove from heat.

Stir in vanilla wafers, walnuts and wine. Shape into 1-inch balls; roll in sugar.

Store Chocolate-Wine Balls in tightly covered cookie jar or metal can. Let stand several days to blend flavors. Flavor improves with age up to 4 weeks.

About 3½ dozen.

Velvet Fudge Soufflé

    ½ cup sugar
    2 envelopes unflavored gelatin
    ¼ teaspoon salt
    1¾ cups sweet red wine
    6 egg yolks
    1 package (12 ounces) semisweet
        chocolate chips
    6 egg whites
    ½ cup sugar
    1½ cups chilled whipping cream
        Sweetened whipped cream

Extend height of 1-quart soufflé dish 3 inches above dish with band of double thickness aluminum foil; secure ends of foil by folding together, taping or fastening with paper clips.

Mix ½ cup sugar, the gelatin, salt and wine in 2-quart saucepan. Beat egg yolks slightly;

stir yolks and chocolate chips into gelatin mixture. Cook over medium heat, stirring constantly, just until mixture boils.

Chill pan in bowl of ice and water or in refrigerator, stirring occasionally, just until mixture mounds slightly when dropped from a spoon, 20 to 30 minutes. Mixture should be slightly thicker than unbeaten egg whites. If mixture becomes too thick, place pan in bowl of hot water, stirring constantly, until mixture is of proper consistency.

Beat egg whites until foamy in large mixer bowl. (Egg whites should be at room temperature when beaten for best volume.) Gradually beat in ½ cup sugar; beat until stiff and glossy. (Do not underbeat.) Fold thickened gelatin mixture into meringue.

Beat 1½ cups cream in chilled small mixer bowl until stiff; fold into meringue mixture. Carefully turn into soufflé dish. Refrigerate until set, about 8 hours.

Just before serving, run knife around inside of foil band and remove band. Garnish soufflé with sweetened whipped cream.

12 to 16 servings.

Velvet Fudge Soufflé is a smooth cold soufflé you can stake your reputation on. Thanks to the gelatin, it never will fall! The flavor, heady and rich, is a product of the marvelous blending of wine, chocolate and cream. The foil collar around the rim assures the high crown that always provokes "ahs" around the table.

Spiced Prunes

1 package (12 ounces) ready-to-eat
  pitted prunes
⅓ cup sweet red wine
¼ cup sugar
4 whole cloves
2-inch cinnamon stick

Pack prunes in pint jar. Heat remaining ingredients in 1-quart saucepan over low heat, stirring constantly, until sugar dissolves; pour over prunes. Cover and refrigerate several days to blend flavors. (Add more wine to cover prunes if necessary.)

1 pint.

Glazed Cherry Tarts

1 cup all-purpose flour*
½ teaspoon salt
⅓ cup plus 1 tablespoon shortening or ⅓
  cup lard
2 to 3 tablespoons cold water
1 tablespoon plus 1½ teaspoons
  cornstarch
⅓ cup sugar
⅛ teaspoon salt
⅛ teaspoon ground cinnamon
1 can (16 ounces) pitted tart red
  cherries, drained (reserve ½ cup
  syrup)
⅔ cup sweet red wine
  Red food color
1 package (3 ounces) cream cheese,
  softened
1 tablespoon sweet red wine
½ cup chilled whipping cream
1 tablespoon sugar

Heat oven to 475°. Measure flour and ½ teaspoon salt into bowl; cut in shortening. Sprinkle in water, 1 tablespoon at a time, mixing until all flour is moistened and pastry almost cleans side of bowl (1 to 2 teaspoons water can be added if necessary).

Gather pastry into ball; shape into flattened round on lightly floured cloth-covered board. Roll pastry into 13-inch circle with floured stockinet-covered rolling pin. Cut circle into 4½-inch rounds; fit rounds over backs of muffin cups or small custard cups, making pleats so pastry will fit closely. (If using individual pie plates or tart pans, cut pastry rounds 1 inch larger than inverted pie plates; fit into pie plates.) Prick all over with fork to prevent puffing. Place on baking sheet. Bake 8 to 10 mintues. Cool tart shells before removing from pans.

Mix cornstarch, ⅓ cup sugar, ⅛ teaspoon salt and the cinnamon in 1½-quart saucepan. Gradually stir in reserved cherry syrup and ⅔ cup wine until mixture is smooth. Cook over medium heat, stirring constantly, until sauce thickens and boils. Boil and stir 1 minute. Remove from heat. Stir in cherries and a few drops of food color.

Beat cream cheese and 1 tablespoon wine in small mixer bowl until light and fluffy. Spread cream cheese mixture evenly in tart shells. Spoon cherries and syrup over cream cheese mixture. Refrigerate until chilled.

Beat cream and 1 tablespoon sugar in chilled small mixer bowl until stiff. Serve tarts with sweetened whipped cream. (Pictured on page 20.)

8 servings.

*If using self-rising flour, omit ½ teaspoon salt. Pie crusts made with self-rising flour differ in flavor and texture from those made with plain flour.

Red Wine Apple Pie

5 cups thinly sliced pared and cored tart
  apples
¾ cup sugar
¼ cup sweet red wine
1 tablespoon lemon juice
¼ cup all-purpose flour
2 tablespoons sugar
⅛ teaspoon salt
3 tablespoons butter or margarine
2 cups all-purpose flour*
1 cup shredded Cheddar cheese (about
  4 ounces)
1 teaspoon salt
⅔ cup plus 2 tablespoons shortening or
  ⅔ cup lard
4 to 5 tablespoons cold water

Place apples, ¾ cup sugar, the wine and lemon juice in 3-quart saucepan. Cover and cook over medium heat, stirring occasionally, until apples are just tender, 7 to 8 minutes.

Mix ¼ cup flour, 2 tablespoons sugar and ⅛ teaspoon salt; stir into apple mixture. Heat to boiling, stirring constantly. Boil and stir 1 minute. Remove from heat. Stir in butter. Cool to room temperature.

Heat oven to 425°. Measure 2 cups flour, the cheese and 1 teaspoon salt into bowl; cut in shortening. Sprinkle in water, 1 tablespoon at a time, mixing until all flour is moistened and pastry almost cleans side of bowl (1 to 2 teaspoons water can be added if necessary).

Gather pastry into ball; divide in half and shape into 2 flattened rounds on lightly floured cloth-covered board. Roll one round 2 inches larger than inverted 8-inch pie plate with floured stockinet-covered rolling pin. Fold pastry into quarters; place in pie plate. Unfold and ease into pie plate.

Turn apple mixture into pastry-lined pie plate. Trim overhanging edge of pastry ½ inch from rim of pie plate. Roll second round of pastry. Fold into quarters; cut slits so steam can escape. Place over filling and unfold. Trim overhanging edge of pastry 1 inch from rim of pie plate. Fold and roll top edge under lower edge, pressing on rim to seal; flute. Cover edge with 2- to 3-inch strip of aluminum foil to prevent excessive browning. Bake 25 to 30 minutes; remove foil. Bake 15 minutes. (Pictured on page 20.)

*If using self-rising flour, omit 1 teaspoon salt. Pie crusts made with self-rising flour differ in flavor and texture from those made with plain flour.

Note: If desired, 1 package (11 ounces) pie crust mix or sticks can be substituted for the pastry.

Fruit and cheese accompanied by a glass of wine are a traditional dessert. Now they have all been combined in that wonderful American favorite—good old-fashioned apple pie. The wine sharpens the taste of the apples, and the cheese accents the tart flavor of the filling. All together they make an incredibly delicious dessert that's irresistible for snacks, too.

COOKING WITH
White Wine

White Wine Main Dishes

Macaroni-Beef Bake

Pasticcio

1 package (7 ounces) long macaroni*
¾ pound ground beef
1 small onion, chopped
½ can (8-ounce size) tomato sauce
½ cup dry white wine
1 teaspoon salt
¼ cup grated kefalotyri, Parmesan or Romano cheese
⅛ teaspoon ground nutmeg
1¼ cups milk
3 tablespoons butter or margarine
2 eggs, beaten
½ cup grated kefalotyri, Parmesan or Romano cheese

Cook macaroni as directed on package; drain.

While macaroni is cooking, cook and stir beef and onion in 10-inch skillet until beef is brown; drain off fat. Stir in tomato sauce, wine and salt. Heat to boiling; reduce heat. Simmer uncovered until liquid is almost absorbed, about 8 minutes.

Heat oven to 350°. Spread half of the macaroni in greased baking dish, 8x8x2 inches; cover with beef mixture. Mix ¼ cup cheese and the nutmeg; sprinkle over beef mixture. Cover with remaining macaroni.

Cook and stir milk and butter in 2-quart saucepan until butter is melted. Remove from heat. Stir at least half the milk mixture gradually into beaten eggs. Mix back into milk mixture in pan; spoon over macaroni. Sprinkle with ½ cup cheese. Bake uncovered until bubbly, 30 to 35 minutes.

4 servings.

*1 package (7 ounces) elbow macaroni can be used.

White Wine Beef and Vegetable Stew is a fine example of cooking *en daube,* which means to braise in an aromatic stock of herbs and wine. Before regulated ovens, special casseroles *(daubières)* were designed with deep lids to hold hot ashes and coals, insuring long, even cooking.

White Wine Beef and Vegetable Stew

Daube de Boeuf

   2 pounds beef round steak, cut into 2½-inch squares 1 inch thick
   1 cup dry white wine
   2 tablespoons brandy
   2 tablespoons olive oil
1½ teaspoons salt
   ¼ teaspoon ground pepper
   ¼ teaspoon dried thyme leaves
   1 bay leaf, crumbled
   2 cloves garlic, minced
1½ cups thinly sliced onions
1½ cups thinly sliced carrots
   ½ pound bacon, cut into 2-inch pieces
   ½ cup all-purpose flour
   5 ounces fresh mushrooms, sliced (about 2 cups)
   2 large tomatoes, peeled and chopped
   1 teaspoon instant beef bouillon

Mix steak, wine, brandy, oil, salt, pepper, thyme, bay leaf, garlic, onions and carrots in 4-quart glass bowl. Cover and refrigerate, stirring frequently, at least 6 hours but no longer than 24 hours.

Heat oven to 325°. Heat 8 cups water to boiling in large kettle. Add bacon and reduce heat. Simmer uncovered 10 minutes; drain on paper towels.

Remove steak from marinade. Strain marinade, reserving vegetables and liquid. Coat steak with flour; shake off excess. Layer half of the bacon and reserved vegetables, the mushrooms, tomatoes and steak in Dutch oven. Top with remaining bacon and vegetables.

Measure reserved marinade liquid; add enough water to measure 1½ cups. Heat liquid and bouillon to boiling; pour over meat and vegetables. Cover and bake until meat is tender, about 3 hours. (Pictured on page 17.)

6 servings.

Barbecued Meat Cubes

Souvlakia

1½ pounds lamb or veal, cut into 1-inch cubes
   ¾ cup dry white wine
   ¼ cup olive oil
   2 tablespoons white wine vinegar
   2 to 3 teaspoons ground oregano
   1 teaspoon salt
   ¼ teaspoon ground pepper
   2 cloves garlic, finely chopped
   1 small onion, chopped

Arrange lamb on six 8-inch skewers; place in shallow glass baking dish. Mix remaining ingredients; pour over meat. Cover tightly and refrigerate, turning occasionally, at least 12 hours but no longer than 24 hours.

Set oven control to broil and/or 550°. Broil 4 inches from heat, turning and basting with marinade every 5 minutes until done, 10 to 15 minutes.

6 main-dish or 12 appetizer servings.

Oxtail Soup

1½ pounds cut-up oxtails
 1 cup sliced celery
 ½ cup finely chopped onion
 1 clove garlic, finely chopped
 1 small bay leaf
 1 teaspoon salt
 ¼ teaspoon ground pepper
 ⅛ teaspoon dried rosemary leaves, crushed
 ⅛ teaspoon dried thyme leaves
 ⅛ teaspoon ground mace
 ⅛ teaspoon ground marjoram
 6 cups water
 ½ cup dry white wine
 ¼ cup dry red wine
 2 tablespoons instant beef bouillon
 2 medium carrots, sliced
 1 small turnip, sliced

Heat oven to 500°. Place oxtails on rack in Dutch oven. Roast uncovered 25 minutes. Remove from oven; remove rack.

Add celery, onion, garlic, bay leaf, salt, pepper, rosemary, thyme, mace and marjoram. Return to oven. Roast uncovered 10 minutes. Remove from oven.

Reduce oven temperature to 350°. Add water, white wine, red wine and instant bouillon to Dutch oven. Cover and bake 2 hours.

Remove from oven.* Skim fat off liquid. If desired, remove meat from bones. Add carrots and turnip. Cover and bake until carrots and turnip are tender, about 30 minutes.

3 servings.

*Soup can be refrigerated no longer than 18 hours at this point. Skim fat off liquid. Remove meat from bones. Stir meat, carrots and turnip into soup. To serve, heat oven to 350°. Bake until carrots and turnip are tender, about 30 minutes.

Marmalade-Glazed Ham

5-pound fully cooked boneless smoked ham
 ½ cup orange marmalade
 ⅓ cup sweet white wine
 1 tablespoon prepared mustard
 ⅛ teaspoon ground cloves

Heat oven to 325°. Place ham fat side up on rack in open shallow roasting pan. Roast uncovered 1 hour. Remove from oven.

Score fat surface of ham lightly into uniform diamond shapes. Mix remaining ingredients; spoon over scored ham. Return to oven. Roast 40 minutes. Remove from oven. Let stand 15 minutes for easier carving.

About 15 servings.

Spicy Sausage

1 pound Polish sausage or Kielbasa, cut into 2-inch pieces
 1 teaspoon instant beef bouillon
 ¼ cup boiling water
 1 cup dry white wine
 1 tablespoon prepared mustard
 ¼ teaspoon ground ginger
 1 cup golden raisins

Heat oven to 400°. Place sausage in ungreased baking dish, 10x6x1½ inches. Dissolve bouillon in boiling water. Stir remaining ingredients into bouillon; pour over sausage. Bake uncovered until done, 25 to 30 minutes.

3 or 4 servings.

Braised Veal Birds

Paupiettes de Veau

1 pound veal round, arm or
   blade steak, ½ inch thick
½ teaspoon salt
⅛ teaspoon ground pepper
1 tablespoon butter or margarine
¼ cup finely chopped onion
¼ cup snipped parsley
4 thin slices cooked ham
4 hard-cooked eggs
2 tablespoons butter or margarine
6 medium carrots, cut into
   julienne strips
8 small white onions
½ cup dry white wine
½ teaspoon instant beef bouillon
½ cup water
2 teaspoons cornstarch
2 tablespoons water
   Mashed potatoes (enough
   for 4 servings)

Cut bone and fat from steak; cut steak into 4 pieces. Pound steak until ¼ inch thick. Sprinkle one side of steak with salt and pepper.

Melt 1 tablespoon butter. Cook and stir onion and parsley in butter over medium heat until onion is tender, 4 to 5 minutes.

Spread equal amount of onion mixture over each piece of steak. Place a slice of ham and an egg on top of each onion mixture. Roll up carefully, beginning at narrow end; tie string around middle and ends of each roll.

Melt 2 tablespoons butter in Dutch oven. Brown veal rolls in butter over medium heat. Add carrots, onions, wine, bouillon and ½ cup water. Cover and bake in 325° oven until meat is tender, about 1 hour.

Remove veal rolls and vegetables from Dutch oven. Remove the strings; cut each roll in half. Keep warm while preparing gravy.

Mix cornstarch and 2 tablespoons water; stir into pan liquid. Heat to boiling, stirring constantly. Boil and stir until gravy thickens, 1 to 2 minutes. For each serving, place 2 halves of each roll in a nest of mashed potatoes. Serve gravy with veal rolls. (Pictured on page 54.)

4 servings.

Many classics in French cooking are named for their garniture, their originator or even the kind of pot they're cooked in. Rolls of meat frequently were named for their shape. In old French recipes, the veal rolls were wrapped in rashers of bacon, and the rolled-up slices resembled big corks—in French, *paupiettes.*

Stuffed Breast of Chicken

2½- to 3-pound broiler-fryer chicken,
    cut up
2 slices white bread
6 sprigs parsley
1 egg, beaten
1 teaspoon salt
¼ teaspoon ground pepper
¼ teaspoon ground savory
2 tablespoons butter or margarine,
    melted
1 teaspoon flour
1 cup dry white wine
½ cup water
1 tablespoon cornstarch
1 teaspoon instant chicken bouillon

Remove skin from chicken drumsticks, thighs, wings and back with sharp knife, reserving thigh skin. Cut meat from thighs, drumsticks, wings and back. Grind cut chicken, bread and parsley through fine blade of meat grinder; mix with egg, salt, pepper and savory.

Heat oven to 400°. Remove chicken breasts from bones. Cut each chicken breast in half. Loosen skin from cut side of each breast half with sharp knife, forming pocket. Fill pocket with stuffing, fold skin down to cover stuffing. Use reserved thigh skin to help cover stuffing if necessary.

Place in buttered baking dish, 10x6x1½ inches. Brush with melted butter; sprinkle with flour. Pour wine over chicken. Bake uncovered until chicken is done, about 35 minutes. Remove chicken to warm platter. Keep warm while preparing sauce.

Pour liquid remaining in baking dish into 1-quart saucepan. Stir water into cornstarch; pour into liquid. Stir in instant bouillon. Heat to boiling over medium heat, stirring constantly. Boil and stir 1 minute. Pour sauce over chicken.

4 servings.

Country-Style Chicken Casserole

Poulet en Cocotte à la Paysanne

2½- to 3-pound broiler-fryer chicken
½ teaspoon salt
⅛ teaspoon ground pepper
2 tablespoons butter or margarine
4 thin strips salt pork
2 tablespoons butter or margarine
8 medium carrots, quartered
8 medium turnips, quartered, or
  8 small whole white onions
1 can (10¾ ounces) condensed
  chicken broth
½ teaspoon salt
⅛ teaspoon ground pepper
½ cup dry white wine
1 tablespoon plus 1½ teaspoons
  cornstarch
3 tablespoons water

Rub skin of chicken with ½ teaspoon salt and ⅛ teaspoon pepper. Fold wings across back with tips touching; tie drumsticks to tail.

Melt 2 tablespoons butter in Dutch oven. Brown chicken in butter over medium heat about 30 minutes. Place 2 strips salt pork over breast and 1 strip lengthwise over each drumstick.

Heat oven to 325°. Melt 2 tablespoons butter in 10-inch skillet. Toss half of the carrots and turnips in butter; place in Dutch oven around chicken. Toss remaining vegetables in butter; place around chicken. Pour broth over chicken and vegetables; sprinkle with ½ teaspoon salt and ⅛ teaspoon pepper. Cover and bake until thickest pieces of chicken are done, about 1¾ hours.

Remove chicken and vegetables to warm platter; remove salt pork strips and string from chicken. Keep chicken warm while preparing sauce.

Stir wine into chicken broth. Heat to boiling, stirring constantly. Boil and stir 3 minutes. Mix cornstarch and water; stir into wine broth. Heat to boiling, stirring constantly. Boil and stir 3 minutes; skim off fat. Serve sauce with chicken.

4 or 5 servings.

Chicken Livers over Rice

½ cup vegetable oil
2 packages (8 ounces each) frozen
  chicken livers, thawed, drained and
  cut in half
¼ teaspoon salt
  Pinch of ground pepper
½ cup sweet white wine
1 can (10½ ounces) beef gravy
2 tablespoons butter or margarine
¼ cup water
1 tablespoon cornstarch
3 to 4 cups hot cooked brown
  or white rice

Heat oil in 10-inch skillet over medium heat. Add livers; sprinkle with salt and pepper. Cook and stir livers in hot oil until brown, about 3 minutes; drain.

Heat wine to boiling in 1½-quart saucepan; reduce heat. Simmer uncovered 1 minute. Stir in gravy and chicken livers. Heat to boiling; reduce heat. Simmer uncovered 5 minutes. Stir in butter until melted. Stir water into cornstarch. Stir cornstarch mixture gradually into sauce. Heat to boiling. Boil and stir 1 minute. Serve over rice.

4 or 5 servings.

Supper Roll-Ups

1 package (10 ounces) frozen asparagus
  spears
2 packages (4 ounces each) sliced turkey
  luncheon meat
1 can (10¾ ounces) condensed cream of
  shimp soup
⅓ cup dry white wine
2 tablespoons chopped almonds

Heat oven to 350°. Cook asparagus spears as directed on package; drain.

Wrap each turkey slice around 2 or 3 asparagus spears. Place in ungreased baking dish, 10x6x1½ inches. Mix soup and wine; pour over turkey. Garnish with almonds. Bake uncovered until bubbly, about 25 minutes.

4 servings.

Creamy Vegetables with Tuna

1 package (8 ounces) frozen mixed
  vegetables with onion sauce
½ cup water
¼ cup dry white wine
1 tablespoon butter or margarine
1 can (6½ ounces) tuna, drained and
  flaked
2 English muffins, split and toasted
  Shredded Cheddar cheese

Heat frozen vegetables, water and wine to boiling in covered 10-inch skillet. Remove from heat. Stir until sauce is smooth. Stir in butter and tuna. Heat over low heat, stirring constantly, until hot and bubbly.

Place muffins cut sides up on ovenproof platter. Spoon tuna-vegetable mixture over muffins; sprinkle with cheese. Set oven control to broil and/or 550°. Broil muffins 5 inches from heat until cheese is melted.

2 servings.

Macaroni and Cheese with Tuna

1 package (7 ounces) elbow macaroni
  (about 2 cups)
1 cup diagonally sliced celery
½ cup sliced pimiento-stuffed olives
1 can (9½ ounces) tuna, drained
2 tablespoons grated onion
1 teaspoon salt
¼ teaspoon ground pepper
3 cups shredded process sharp
  American cheese (about 12 ounces)
2 tablespoons butter or margarine
1 tablespoon flour
½ teaspoon salt
¼ teaspoon ground pepper
1 cup dairy sour cream
1 cup dry white wine
1 tablespoon butter or margarine

Cook macaroni as directed on package; drain and rinse. Stir in celery and olives into macaroni.

Heat oven to 375°. Place half of the macaroni mixture in ungreased baking dish, 13x9x2 inches. Mix tuna, onion, 1 teaspoon salt, ¼ teaspoon pepper and the cheese. Sprinkle macaroni mixture with half of the tuna mixture; repeat.

Melt 2 tablespoons butter in 2-quart saucepan over low heat; stir in flour, ½ teaspoon salt and ¼ teaspoon pepper. Cook over low heat, stirring constantly, until mixture is smooth and bubbly. Remove from heat. Stir in sour cream and wine. Heat to boiling, stirring constantly. Pour over tuna mixture; dot with 1 tablespoon butter. Cover with aluminum foil and bake 30 minutes. Uncover; bake until golden, about 15 minutes.

8 to 10 servings.

Nothing is better suited to wine than fish! And there are hundreds of recipes for sole. Whether you cook a true European sole (rex, Dover, English) or an American near-kin (sand dab, lemon or gray sole), the texture will be firm but light and flaky and the flavor delicate.

Sole with Green Grapes

Filets de Sole Véronique

2 tablespoons finely chopped shallots
2 pounds fresh or frozen (thawed)
   sole fillets
1 teaspoon salt
¼ teaspoon ground pepper
1 cup dry white wine
1 tablespoon lemon juice
1 can (16 ounces) seedless green grapes,
   drained (reserve liquid)
2 tablespoons butter or margarine
2 tablespoons flour
½ cup whipping cream
2 tablespoons butter or margarine

Sprinkle shallots in 10-inch skillet.* Sprinkle fillets with salt and pepper. Fold in half; arrange in skillet. Add wine, lemon juice and reserved grape liquid. Heat to boiling; reduce heat. Cover and simmer until fillets flake easily, 4 to 5 minutes. Remove fillets with slotted spatula to oven-proof platter; keep warm.

Add grapes to liquid in skillet. Heat to boiling; reduce heat. Simmer uncovered 3 minutes. Remove grapes with slotted spoon.

Heat liquid in skillet to boiling; boil until reduced to 1 cup. Melt 2 tablespoons butter. Stir in flour. Stir flour mixture, a small amount at a time, into reduced liquid. Cook over low heat, stirring constantly, until thickened. Remove from heat. Stir in cream. Heat to boiling. Add 2 tablespoons butter; stir until melted. Drain excess liquid from platter if necessary. Spoon sauce over fillets.

Set oven control to broil and/or 550°. Broil fillets just until sauce is glazed, about 3 minutes. Garnish with grapes.

6 to 8 servings.

*Use pyrosyran, non-stick finish, enamel or stainless steel (not aluminum).

Baked Fish, Greek Style

Spetsioteko Psari

¼ cup olive oil
½ cup dry bread crumbs
2 pounds fresh or frozen (thawed)
   red snapper fillets*
1 teaspoon salt
¼ cup lemon juice
½ cup olive oil
¼ cup tomato sauce
1 cup snipped parsley
½ cup dry white wine
2 cloves garlic, finely chopped
1 teaspoon salt
¼ teaspoon ground pepper
½ cup dry bread crumbs

Heat oven to 350°. Pour ¼ cup oil into baking dish, 13x9x2 inches. Sprinkle ½ cup crumbs over oil. Place fillets in single layer in baking dish; sprinkle with 1 teaspoon salt. Pour lemon juice on top.

Mix ½ cup oil, the tomato sauce, parsley, wine, garlic, 1 teaspoon salt and the pepper; spoon over fillets. Sprinkle with ½ cup crumbs. Bake uncovered until golden brown, about 40 minutes.

6 servings.

*2 pounds fresh or frozen (thawed) cod, haddock, halibut or yellow pike fillets can be substituted for the red snapper fillets.

Artists have long considered the scallop shell to be one of nature's loveliest forms. And we've filled these *coquilles* beautifully! Rich and flavorful, with a hint of the sea. Buttery bread crumbs sprinkled over the cheese are a traditional touch.

Scallops and Mushrooms in Wine Sauce

Coquilles Saint-Jacques à la Parisienne

  2 packages (12 ounces each) frozen
    scallops (about 6 cups)
  1 small white onion, chopped
  ¼ cup snipped parsley
    About 2 cups dry white wine
  2 tablespoons butter or margarine
  5 ounces fresh mushroom caps, sliced
    (about 2 cups)
  1 shallot, chopped
  3 tablespoons butter or margarine
  2 tablespoons flour
  2 tablespoons whipping cream
  ¾ cup grated Gruyère cheese
    (about 4 ounces)
  2 tablespoons butter or margarine
  1 cup soft bread crumbs

Place frozen scallops, onion and parsley in 3-quart saucepan. Add enough wine to barely cover scallops. Heat to boiling; reduce heat. Simmer uncovered until scallops are tender, about 8 minutes.

Drain scallops, reserving liquid. Heat reserved liquid to boiling. Boil until reduced to 1 cup, about 30 minutes; strain and reserve.

Melt 2 tablespoons butter in 8-inch skillet. Cook and stir mushrooms and shallot in butter until shallot is tender, about 6 minutes; reserve.

Melt 3 tablespoons butter in 1½-quart saucepan. Remove from heat. Stir in flour and reserved scallop-wine liquid; beat until smooth. Cook over low heat, stirring constantly, until sauce is medium thick. Remove from heat. Stir in cream, scallops, mushrooms and ¼ cup of the cheese.

Spoon mixture into 5 buttered individual baking shells or ramekins. Sprinkle scallop mixture with remaining cheese. Set oven control to broil and/or 550°. Broil shells 5 inches from heat until bubbly, 4 to 5 minutes.

Melt 2 tablespoons butter; toss bread crumbs in butter. Sprinkle shells with crumbs. Broil until crumbs are toasted.

5 servings.

Shrimp-Cheese Bake

  6 eggs
2½ cups milk
  ½ cup dry white wine
  2 tablespoons snipped parsley
  ¾ teaspoon dry mustard
  ½ teaspoon salt
 10 slices white bread (crusts removed),
    cut into ¼-inch cubes
  2 cups shredded process sharp
    American cheese (about 8 ounces)
  2 cans (4½ ounces each) small shrimp,
    drained

Heat oven to 325°. Beat eggs, milk, wine, parsley, mustard and salt with rotary beater. Stir in remaining ingredients. Pour into ungreased baking dish, 12x7½x2 inches. Bake uncovered until center is set, about 1 hour.

8 servings.

Sauced Shrimp

Garides me Saltsa

2 quarts water
1 medium onion, sliced
1 lemon, sliced
1½ teaspoons salt
1 teaspoon mixed pickling spice
1 package (12 ounces) frozen
   quick-cooking peeled shrimp
1 tablespoon olive oil
1 cup grated onion
1 can (16 ounces) whole tomatoes
¾ cup dry white wine
2 tablespoons snipped parsley
1 bay leaf
1 teaspoon salt
¼ teaspoon ground pepper
3 to 4 cups cooked rice or bulgur

Heat water, onion slices, lemon, 1½ teaspoons salt and the pickling spice to boiling in Dutch oven. Add frozen shrimp. Heat to boiling. Remove from heat. Let stand 3 minutes; drain. Remove shrimp from onion-spice mixture; reserve shrimp.

Heat oil in 10-inch skillet. Cook and stir grated onion in hot oil until tender. Stir in tomatoes, wine, parsley, bay leaf, 1 teaspoon salt and the pepper. Heat to boiling; reduce heat. Simmer uncovered 15 minutes. Add reserved shrimp; heat through. Serve over rice. (Pictured on page 53.)

4 servings.

Manhattan Clam Linguine

2 quarts plus 3½ cups water
1 can (8 ounces) minced clams, drained
   (reserve liquor)
1 tablespoon salt
1 package (7 or 8 ounces)
   linguine or spaghetti
2 tablespoons butter or margarine
2 tablespoons snipped parsley
3 cloves garlic, finely chopped
1½ teaspoons dried sweet basil leaves
¼ teaspoon dried thyme leaves
   Dash of ground pepper
½ cup whipping cream
¼ cup dry white wine
¼ cup grated Parmesan cheese
2 tablespoons butter or margarine,
   softened
¼ teaspoon salt

Heat water, reserved clam liquor and 1 tablespoon salt to boiling in large kettle or Dutch oven. Add linguine gradually. Boil uncovered, stirring occasionally, *just* until tender, 8 to 10 minutes; drain.

While lingine is cooking, prepare sauce. Melt 2 tablespoons butter in 2-quart saucepan. Stir in parsley, garlic, basil, thyme, pepper, and clams. Cook and stir over low heat until clams are heated through. Heat cream and wine to boiling in 1½-quart saucepan over low heat, stirring constantly. Boil and stir 1 minute; pour over clam mixture.

Transfer hot linguine to warm platter. Pour sauce over linguine. Toss linquine and sauce with remaining ingredients until well mixed.

3 or 4 servings.

Bacon-Cheese Pie

Quiche Lorraine

⅔ cup dry white wine
⅓ cup finely chopped onion
1 cup all-purpose flour*
½ teaspoon salt
⅓ cup plus 1 tablespoon shortening
   or ⅓ cup lard
2 to 3 tablespoons cold water
12 slices bacon (about ½ pound),
   crisply fried and crumbled
1 cup shredded natural Swiss cheese
   (about 4 ounces)
4 eggs
1½ cups half-and-half
¾ teaspoon salt
¼ teaspoon sugar
⅛ teaspoon ground cayenne red
   pepper

Heat wine and onion to boiling in 1½-quart saucepan; reduce heat. Simmer uncovered 2 minutes. Remove from heat. Cool to room temperature.

Heat oven to 425°. Measure flour and ½ teaspoon salt into bowl; cut in shortening. Sprinkle in water, 1 tablespoon at a time, mixing until all flour is moistened and pastry almost cleans side of bowl (1 to 2 teaspoons water can be added if necessary). Gather pastry into ball; shape into flattened round on lightly floured cloth-covered board. Roll pastry 2 inches larger than inverted 9-inch pie plate with floured stockinet-covered rolling pin. Fold pastry into quarters; place in pie plate. Unfold and ease into pie plate. Trim overhanging edge of pastry 1 inch from rim of pie plate. Fold and roll pastry under, even with pie plate; flute.

Sprinkle bacon and cheese into pastry-lined pie plate. Beat eggs slightly. Beat in wine mixture and remaining ingredients; pour into pie plate. Bake 15 minutes.

Reduce oven temperature to 300°. Bake until knife inserted 1 inch from edge comes out clean, about 30 minutes. Remove from oven; let stand 10 minutes before cutting. Serve in wedges.

6 servings.

*If using self-rising flour, omit salt.

Cheesy Eggs with Wine

2 eggs
1 tablespoon water
1 tablespoon dry white wine
⅛ teaspoon salt
   Dash of ground pepper
2 tablespoons shredded Cheddar,
   Monterey (Jack) or Swiss cheese
½ tablespoon butter or margarine

Mix eggs, water, wine, salt and pepper with fork. Stir in cheese.

Heat butter in skillet over medium heat until just hot enough to sizzle a drop of water. Pour egg mixture into skillet. As mixture begins to set, gently lift cooked portion with spatula so that uncooked portion can flow to bottom. Cook until eggs are thickened but still moist, 3 to 5 minutes.

1 serving.

Cheese Spaghetti Toss

Spaghetti alla Carbonara

1 package (16 ounces) thin spaghetti
½ pound bacon, cut into ½-inch squares
½ cup dry white wine or
  dry vermouth
3 eggs, well beaten
1 cup freshly grated Romano or
  Parmesan cheese
  Freshly ground pepper

Cook spaghetti as directed on package; drain but do not rinse. Return to kettle.

While spaghetti is cooking, fry bacon over medium heat until almost crisp; remove bacon and drain on paper towels.

Stir wine into hot bacon fat. Heat to boiling. Boil and stir 3 minutes. Mix bacon, wine and bacon fat with spaghetti.

Add eggs and ½ cup of the cheese; toss over low heat until egg adheres to spaghetti and appears cooked. Serve with remaining cheese and freshly ground pepper.

4 servings.

Welsh Rabbit

¼ cup butter or margarine
¼ cup all-purpose flour
½ teaspoon salt
¼ teaspoon ground pepper
¼ teaspoon dry mustard
¼ teaspoon Worcestershire sauce
1 cup milk
½ cup medium white wine
2 cups shredded Cheddar cheese
  (about 8 ounces)
4 slices toast

Melt butter in 2-quart saucepan over low heat. Stir in flour, salt, pepper, mustard and Worcestershire sauce. Cook over low heat, stirring constantly, until smooth and bubbly. Remove from heat. Stir in milk. Heat to boiling, stirring constantly. Boil and stir 1 minute.

Gradually stir wine into sauce mixture; stir in cheese. Heat over low heat, stirring constantly, until cheese is melted. Serve over toast. Sprinkle with paprika if desired.

4 servings.

Cheese Fondue

8 ounces Swiss cheese,* diced
8 ounces Gruyère cheese, diced
2 tablespoons flour
1 clove garlic, halved
2 cups dry white wine
1 tablespoon lemon juice
3 tablespoons kirsch
French bread, cut into 1-inch cubes

Place cheese in plastic bag; sprinkle with flour. Toss until cheese is coated.

Rub cut clove of garlic on bottom and side of 3-quart saucepan; add wine. Heat over low heat just until bubbles rise to surface (wine must not boil). Stir in lemon juice; add cheese, about ½ cup at a time, stirring constantly with wooden spoon. Stir until cheese is melted. Stir in kirsch.

Pour into ceramic fondue pot over low heat. Use long-handled forks to spear bread cubes; then dip and swirl in fondue with stirring motion.

4 servings.

*The Swiss cheese should be natural (not process) and aged at least 6 months.

Dipping foods into the same pot is an ancient symbol of good fellowship and trust. And a rich cheese fondue is certain to win friends. It never fails to evoke a warm and festive atmosphere. Especially welcome after frosty sports.

Cream of Cheese Soup

2 tablespoons butter or margarine
3 green onions (with tops), thinly sliced
½ cup thinly sliced celery
1¼ cups water
½ cup half-and-half
⅔ cup pasteurized process cheese spread
1 teaspoon instant chicken bouillon
⅛ teaspoon ground nutmeg
⅓ cup dry white wine
Paprika
Toasted croutons

Melt butter in 3-quart saucepan over medium heat. Cook and stir onions and celery in butter until onions are tender, about 8 minutes.

Stir in water, half-and-half, cheese spread, instant bouillon and nutmeg. Heat to boiling over medium heat, stirring constantly; stir in wine. Heat to boiling. Boil and stir 1 minute. Sprinkle each serving with paprika and garnish with croutons.

3 servings.

Salmon Steak Bake (page 27), Sauced Shrimp (page 49) and Tangy Tomato Fish (page 28).

Braised Veal Birds (page 43) are adapted from the classic French recipe *paupiettes de veau*.

Broccoli Puff (page 59), California Artichokes (page 58) and Glazed Carrots (page 60).

Dessert Wine Jelly (page 64)—a truly elegant do-ahead dessert for the busy cook.

White Wine Side Dishes

Blue Cheese Dip

- 1 package (4 ounces) blue cheese
- 1 package (8 ounces) cream cheese, softened
- ⅓ cup sweet white wine
- 1 tablespoon snipped parsley
- 1 teaspoon Worcestershire sauce
  Dash of garlic powder
- 2 tablespoons snipped parsley

Mix blue cheese and cream cheese in small mixer bowl; stir in wine gradually. Beat until light and fluffy. Beat in 1 tablespoon parsley, the Worcestershire sauce and garlic powder.

Cover and refrigerate until ready to serve. Garnish with 2 tablespoons parsley.

2 cups.

Zippy Cheese Spread

- 1 jar (8 ounces) pasteurized process cheese spread
- 2 tablespoons dry white wine
- 2 tablespoons butter or margarine, softened
- 2 teaspoons prepared mustard
- ½ teaspoon Worcestershire sauce
  Dash of ground cayenne red pepper
  Toast rounds or crackers

Beat all ingredients except toast rounds in small mixer bowl (cheese bits will remain in spread). Serve with toast rounds.

1¼ cups.

California Artichokes

4 artichokes
1 tablespoon olive oil
1 small onion, finely chopped
1 clove garlic, finely chopped
2 teaspoons salt
⅛ teaspoon dried savory leaves
⅛ teaspoon dried thyme leaves
2 cups dry white wine

Remove any discolored leaves and the small leaves at base of each artichoke; trim stem even with base. Cutting straight across, slice 1 inch off top and discard. Snip off points of remaining leaves with scissors. Rinse artichokes under cold running water.

Combine oil, onion, garlic, salt, savory and thyme in Dutch oven. Place artichokes upright in Dutch oven; pour wine over artichokes. Heat to boiling; reduce heat. Cover and simmer until bottoms of artichokes are tender when pierced with knife, about 1 hour.

Remove artichokes carefully from Dutch oven with tongs or 2 large spoons. Place upright on individual serving plates. Accompany each serving with small cup of wine liquid for dipping leaves. (Pictured on page 55.)

4 servings.

Artichokes may look rather awesome, but they are really quite easy to eat. Just pluck a leaf, dip the meaty base in sauce, then pull it between your teeth. After you have eaten the meaty portions of the leaves, pull out the center cone of leaves, slice off the thistlelike covering of the heart and eat.

Cauliflower with Cheese Sauce

1 medium head cauliflower
  (about 2 pounds)
2 tablespoons butter or margarine
2 tablespoons flour
1 teaspoon dry mustard
¼ teaspoon salt
¼ teaspoon ground pepper
½ cup half-and-half
½ cup dry white wine
1 cup shredded process sharp
  American cheese (about 4 ounces)

Heat 1 inch salted water (½ teaspoon salt to 1 cup water) to boiling; add cauliflower. Cover and heat to boiling. Cook until tender, 20 to 25 minutes; drain.

Melt butter in 8-inch skillet over low heat. Stir in flour, mustard, salt and pepper. Cook over low heat, stirring constantly, until mixture is smooth and bubbly. Remove from heat.

Stir in half-and-half and wine (mixture may appear to curdle slightly at first). Heat to boiling, stirring constantly. Boil and stir 1 minute. Stir in cheese. Cook and stir over low heat until cheese is melted. Pour sauce over hot cauliflower. Sprinkle with paprika if desired.

4 to 6 servings.

Broccoli Puff

1 package (10 ounces) frozen chopped
  broccoli
¼ cup butter or margarine
¼ cup all-purpose flour
¼ teaspoon salt
⅛ teaspoon ground pepper
¾ cup milk
¼ cup dry white wine
1 teaspoon instant minced onion
1 teaspoon salt
3 eggs, separated
¼ teaspoon cream of tartar

Cook broccoli as directed on package;
drain.

Heat oven to 350°. Butter 1-quart soufflé
dish. Melt butter over low heat. Stir in flour,
¼ teaspoon salt and the pepper. Cook over
low heat, stirring constantly, until smooth
and bubbly. Remove from heat.

Stir in milk and wine. Heat to boiling, stirring constantly. Boil and stir 1 minute.

Remove from heat. Stir in onion and 1
teaspoon salt.

Beat egg whites and cream of tartar in large
mixer bowl until stiff, about 5 minutes. Beat
yolks in small mixer bowl until thick and
lemon colored, about 4 minutes. Stir egg
yolks into sauce mixture. Stir in broccoli.

Stir about ¼ of the egg whites into the sauce
mixture; gently fold into remaining egg
whites. Carefully pour into soufflé dish. Set
dish in pan of water (1 inch deep).

Bake until puffed and golden and knife inserted halfway between edge and center
comes out clean, about 60 minutes. Serve
immediately. (Pictured on page 55.)

4 to 6 servings.

Glazed Carrots

Carottes Glacées

¼ cup butter or margarine
1 pound carrots, cut into julienne strips
1 cup dry white wine
1 cup water
2 tablespoons sugar
1 teaspoon salt
  Snipped parsley

Melt butter in 10-inch skillet; add carrots, wine, water, sugar and salt. Heat to boiling. Cook uncovered over medium heat until carrots are crisp-tender and only butter-sugar mixture remains, about 40 minutes. Garnish with parsley. (Pictured on page 55.)

6 servings.

Note: If carrots are crisp-tender and extra liquid remains, remove carrots with slotted spoon. Continue cooking liquid until only butter-sugar mixture remains. Return carrots to skillet; cook until carrots are glazed, about 2 minutes.

Creamed Peas
and Shredded Carrots

1 package (10 ounces) frozen green peas and pearl onions
2 tablespoons butter or margarine
2 tablespoons flour
½ teaspoon salt
⅛ teaspoon ground pepper
1¼ cups half-and-half
⅓ cup dry white wine
1½ cups shredded carrots

Cook peas and onions as directed on package; drain.

Melt butter in 10-inch skillet over low heat. Stir in flour, salt and pepper. Cook, stirring constantly, until mixture is smooth and bubbly. Remove from heat.

Stir in cream and wine. Heat to boiling, stirring constantly. Boil and stir 1 minute. Stir in peas and onions and carrots. Cook, stirring occasionally, 5 minutes.

4 to 6 servings.

Potatoes Gourmet

2 pounds potatoes
4 slices bacon
¼ teaspoon instant beef bouillon
  Vegetable oil
⅓ cup dry white wine
2 tablespoons white wine vinegar
1 tablespoon snipped parsley
2 teaspoons snipped chives
1 teaspoon salt
1 teaspoon dried tarragon leaves
¾ teaspoon ground pepper
½ teaspoon dried chervil leaves

Heat 1 inch salted water (½ teaspoon salt to 1 cup water) to boiling; add unpared potatoes. Cover and heat to boiling. Cook until tender, 30 to 35 minutes.

Drain potatoes; cool slightly. Peel potatoes and cut into ¼-inch slices.

Fry bacon in 10-inch skillet until crisp; remove bacon and drain on paper towels. Cool and crumble. Dissolve instant bouillon in hot bacon fat. Measure bacon fat and add enough vegetable oil to measure ½ cup. Stir in crumbled bacon and remaining ingredients; mix well.

Pour dressing over warm potatoes; toss until potatoes are coated.

4 to 6 servings.

Lyonnaise Potatoes

3 tablespoons butter or margarine
4 medium potatoes, thinly sliced
1 medium onion, thinly sliced
1 teaspoon salt
⅛ teaspoon ground pepper
½ teaspoon instant chicken bouillon
⅓ cup boiling water
⅓ cup dry white wine
½ teaspoon dried thyme leaves
2 tablespoons snipped parsley

Melt butter in 10-inch skillet over low heat. Cook potatoes, onion, salt and pepper in butter, turning frequently, until potatoes are light brown.

Dissolve instant bouillon in boiling water. Add dissolved bouillon, wine and thyme to potatoes. Heat to boiling; reduce heat. Cover and simmer, stirring occasionally, until liquid is absorbed and potatoes are tender, about 13 minutes. Stir in parsley.

4 or 5 servings.

Wine Sauerkraut

Weinkraut

2 tablespoons butter or margarine
2 cans (16 ounces each) sauerkraut, drained
1⅓ cups dry white wine

Melt butter in 10-inch skillet over low heat; add sauerkraut. Cover and cook, stirring occasionally, 30 minutes; add wine. Heat to boiling; reduce heat. Cover and simmer until liquid is absorbed, about 45 minutes.

5 or 6 servings.

Note: This is a mild variation of sauerkraut. Fresh sauerkraut can be used. Follow directions above except—simmer until liquid is absorbed, about 1 hour.

Acorn Squash Bake

2 acorn squash, cut in half
½ teaspoon salt
4 tablespoons butter or margarine
⅓ cup dry white wine
⅓ cup honey

Heat oven to 400°. Cut thin slices from bottoms of squash halves so they will stand upright. Place in ungreased baking dish, 13x9x2 inches. Sprinkle cut sides of squash with salt. Place 1 tablespoon butter in each squash cavity.

Mix wine and honey; pour into squash cavities, filling each about ¾ full. Bake uncovered until tender, about 60 minutes.

4 servings.

Vegetable Marinade

1 package (10 ounces) frozen cauliflower
1 cucumber, pared and sliced
1 tomato, cut into wedges
⅓ cup vegetable oil
¼ cup dry white wine
2 tablespoons lemon juice
½ teaspoon salt
¼ teaspoon ground pepper
⅛ teaspoon garlic salt
Lettuce cups

Cook cauliflower as directed on package; drain and refrigerate until chilled.

Place cauliflower, cucumber and tomato in bowl. Mix oil, wine, lemon juice, salt, pepper and garlic salt; pour over vegetables. Cover and refrigerate, stirring occasionally, at least 12 hours but no longer than 24 hours. Serve in lettuce cups.

4 to 6 servings.

Wilted Romaine-Onion Salad

1 medium onion, thinly sliced
  and separated into rings
4 to 6 cups bite-size pieces romaine
⅓ cup vegetable oil
3 tablespoons dry white wine
1 tablespoon sugar
1 teaspoon instant beef bouillon
  Dash of red pepper sauce
  Grated Parmesan or Swiss cheese
  Seasoned croutons

Toss onion rings and romaine in 4 in-dividual salad bowls. Heat oil, wine, sugar, bouillon and red pepper sauce to boiling, stirring occasionally. Drizzle hot dressing on salads; sprinkle with cheese and croutons.

4 servings.

Pepper Sauce

Cut 3 red chili peppers lengthwise in half; remove stems and seeds. Pack peppers in pint jar; pour in enough dry white wine to fill jar. Cover and refrigerate several days to blend flavors. Use as a substitute for vinegar.

1 pint.

Lettuce Wedges with Avocado Dressing

1 ripe avocado
¼ cup dairy sour cream
1 tablespoon lemon juice
¾ teaspoon onion salt
¼ teaspoon Worcestershire sauce
⅓ cup crumbled blue cheese
  (about 2½ ounces)
⅓ cup vegetable oil
¼ cup medium white wine
¼ cup white wine vinegar
  Lettuce wedges

Cut avocado lengthwise in half; remove pit. Scoop out fruit; mash. Stir in sour cream, lemon juice, onion salt and Worcestershire sauce.

Mash cheese with fork; stir in oil, wine and vinegar. Mix with avocado mixture. Cover and refrigerate until chilled, at least 2 hours. Serve over lettuce wedges.

8 servings.

Lemon Dressing for Fruit Salad

⅓ cup frozen lemonade or limeade
  concentrate, thawed
⅓ cup dry white wine
¼ cup vegetable oil
2 tablespoons honey
1 teaspoon poppy seed
  Fruit salad

Beat all ingredients except fruit salad with rotary beater. Serve with your favorite fruit salad.

1 cup.

White Wine Desserts

Orange Dessert Ring with Fruit

2 cups boiling water
2 packages (3 ounces each) orange-flavored gelatin
1 can (16 or 17 ounces) peeled whole apricots, drained (reserve syrup), pitted and halved
Cold water
⅔ cup sweet white wine
1 cup seedless green grapes
1 banana

Pour boiling water on gelatin; stir until gelatin is dissolved. Measure reserved apricot syrup; add enough cold water to measure 1 cup. Stir syrup-water mixture and wine into gelatin. Pour into 4-cup ring mold. Refrigerate until firm, at least 5 hours.

Mix apricot halves and grapes. Cover and refrigerate. Just before serving, dice banana; stir into apricot halves and grapes. Unmold gelatin; fill center and garnish side of ring with fruit.

8 or 9 servings.

White Wine Mold

¾ cup sugar
2 envelopes unflavored gelatin
1 cup dry white wine
1 can (6 ounces) frozen orange juice concentrate, thawed
2 cups water
2 tablespoons lemon juice
Grated peel of 1 lemon
2 cups whipping cream, whipped
Orange slices

Mix sugar and gelatin in 3-quart saucepan; stir in wine, orange juice concentrate, water and lemon juice. Heat to boiling, stirring constantly. Boil and stir 1 minute. Remove from heat. Stir in lemon peel. Refrigerate until mixture mounds slightly when dropped from spoon, about 2½ hours.

Fold chilled gelatin mixture into whipped cream. Pour into 7-cup mold. Refrigerate until firm, about 12 hours. Unmold and garnish with orange slices.

10 to 12 servings.

Dessert Wine Jelly

Weingelee

4 envelopes unflavored gelatin
2 cups cold water
1 cup sugar
3 cups boiling white or red
  grape juice
1 cup medium dry white wine
  Sweetened whipped cream
  Strawberries

Sprinkle gelatin on cold water to soften. Stir in sugar and grape juice; stir until gelatin is dissolved. Stir in wine. Pour into 6-cup mold. Refrigerate until firm, at least 4 hours. Unmold and serve with whipped cream. Garnish with strawberries. (Pictured on page 56.)

8 to 10 servings.

Fruited Dessert Ring

1 can (16 ounces) pear halves,
  drained (reserve syrup)
  Boiling water
2 packages (3 ounces each)
  lime-flavored gelatin
1 cup sweet white wine

Heat reserved pear syrup to boiling; add enough boiling water to measure 1½ cups. Pour boiling liquid on gelatin; stir until gelatin is dissolved. Stir in wine. Refrigerate uncovered until gelatin begins to thicken, about 1½ hours.

Cut pear halves into ½-inch pieces; fold into thickened gelatin. Pour into 6-cup ring mold. Refrigerate until firm, at least 2½ hours; unmold.

7 or 8 servings.

Sauterne Sherbet

Sorbet au Sauterne

2 teaspoons unflavored gelatin
½ cup sugar
1 cup water
⅛ teaspoon salt
1 cup dry sauterne or other dry
  white wine
2 tablespoons lemon juice
1 cup sugar
½ cup water
⅛ teaspoon cream of tartar
2 egg whites

Mix gelatin and ½ cup sugar in 2-quart saucepan. Stir in 1 cup water and the salt. Heat to boiling, stirring constantly. Boil and stir 5 minutes. Remove from heat. Stir in wine and lemon juice. Cool to room temperature. Pour into ice cube tray. Freeze until mushy and partially frozen, about 1 hour 20 minutes.

Heat 1 cup sugar, ½ cup water and the cream of tartar to boiling in 1½-quart saucepan over medium heat, stirring constantly. Boil, without stirring, to 240° on candy thermometer. Beat egg whites in small mixer bowl until soft peaks form. Continue beating while pouring hot syrup in thin stream into egg whites. Beat until mixture is cool, about 8 minutes.

Spoon partially frozen mixture into chilled large mixer bowl. Beat with rotary beater until fluffy; fold in egg white mixture. Pour into ungreased baking pan, 9x9x2 inches. Freeze until firm, about 3 hours. Serve in chilled sherbet glasses.

9 servings.

Frozen Custard

Tortoni

2 egg yolks
½ cup powdered sugar
3 tablespoons dry sherry or
   dry white wine
½ teaspoon vanilla
2 egg whites
1 cup whipping cream, whipped
¾ cup ground dry macaroons
¼ cup maraschino cherries,
   drained and chopped
¼ cup ground dry macaroons

Beat egg yolks and sugar in small mixer bowl until very thick and lemon colored, about 5 minutes. Stir in wine and vanilla.

Beat egg whites in small mixer bowl until stiff but not dry. Fold egg yolk mixture into egg whites. Fold in whipped cream. Stir in ¾ cup macaroons and the cherries. Pour mixture by ⅓ cupfuls into paper liners in muffin cups. Sprinkle with ¼ cup macaroons. Freeeze until firm, about 3½ hours. Freeze any leftover dessert.

11 servings.

Wine-flavored Custard

Zabaglione

6 egg yolks
½ cup sugar
⅓ cup sweet Marsala or
   medium white wine

Beat egg yolks with electric mixer in top of double boiler until foamy. Beat in sugar gradually.

Pour just enough hot water in bottom of double boiler so that top part does not touch water. (Water in double boiler should not boil.) Cook egg yolks over medium heat; mix in wine slowly, beating on high speed until smooth, pale and thick enough to stand in soft mounds. Serve immediately in shallow stemmed glasses.

6 servings.

Variation

Cold Zabaglione: After mixture stands in soft mounds, place top of double boiler in large bowl filled with crushed ice. Beat on high speed until mixture is cold, about 6 minutes. Serve immediately over fresh fruit, such as strawberries or peaches.

As English as the Union Jack, trifle is one of many pudding dishes favored by the British. We've shortcut the traditional recipe by using prepared ladyfingers, a boon for busy cooks. Trifle is at its best when prepared in a glass bowl so the richly colored layers are visible. Spectacular!

Raspberry-Custard Bowl

Trifle

½ cup sugar
3 tablespoons cornstarch
¼ teaspoon salt
3 cups milk
½ cup dry sherry or dry white wine
3 egg yolks, beaten
3 tablespoons butter or margarine, softened*
1 tablespoon vanilla
1 package (2½ ounces) whole blanched almonds
2 packages (3 ounces each) ladyfingers
½ cup red raspberry preserves
1 package (12 ounces) frozen red raspberries, partially thawed (reserve 10 raspberries for garnish)
1 cup chilled whipping cream
2 tablespoons sugar

Mix ½ cup sugar, the cornstarch and salt in 3-quart saucepan; gradually stir in milk and wine. Heat to boiling over medium heat, stirring constantly. Boil and stir 1 minute. Gradually stir at least half of the hot mixture into egg yolks; stir back into hot mixture in pan. Boil and stir 1 minute. Remove from heat. Stir in butter and vanilla until butter melts. Cover and refrigerate at least 3 hours.

Soak almonds in hot water about 3 minutes; drain. Carefully cut almonds lengthwise in half with sharp knife.

Split ladyfingers lengthwise in half; spread each half with raspberry preserves. Layer in 2-quart serving bowl ¼ of the ladyfingers (cut sides up), ¼ cup of the halved almonds, half of the raspberries and half of the pudding; repeat. Arrange remaining ladyfingers around edge of bowl in upright position with cut sides toward center. (It may be necessary to gently ease ladyfingers down into pudding about 1 inch so that they remain upright.) Cover and refrigerate 30 minutes.

Beat cream and 2 tablespoons sugar in chilled small mixer bowl until stiff; spread over top of dessert. Garnish with remaining almonds and reserved raspberries.

8 to 10 servings.

*Do not use soft-type margarine in this recipe.

Broiled Grapefruit

1 grapefruit
1 tablespoon sweet white wine
1 tablespoon honey

Cut grapefruit in half; remove seeds. Cut around edges and sections to loosen; remove centers. Set oven control to broil and/or 550°. Mix wine and honey; pour over grapefruit halves. Place on rack in broiler pan. Broil grapefruit halves 4 to 6 inches from heat until juice bubbles and edges of peel are light brown, 5 to 10 minutes.

2 servings.

Peaches in Wine

¼ cup sugar
¼ cup sweet white wine
1 tablespoon lemon juice
1 can (16 ounces) sliced peaches, drained, or 3 medium peaches, peeled and sliced

Heat sugar, wine and lemon juice in 1½-quart saucepan over medium heat until sugar is dissolved; pour over peaches. Cover and refrigerate, stirring occasionally, until chilled, about 1 hour.

4 servings.

Almond Cream Pie

1½ cups vanilla wafer crumbs
 ¼ cup finely chopped toasted
   slivered almonds
 ¼ cup butter or margarine, melted
 1 envelope unflavored gelatin
 ¼ cup sugar
 ¼ cup all-purpose flour
 ⅛ teaspoon salt
 2 eggs, separated
 ⅔ cup milk
 ½ cup medium white wine
 2 tablespoons medium white wine
 1 cup vanilla wafer crumbs
 1 cup chilled whipping cream
 1 cup chilled whipping cream
 3 tablespoons sugar
   Toasted slivered almonds

Heat oven to 350°. Mix 1½ cups wafer crumbs and the chopped almonds; stir in melted butter. Press crumb mixture firmly and evenly against bottom and side of 9-inch pie plate. Bake 10 minutes; cool.

Mix gelatin, ¼ cup sugar, the flour and salt in 2-quart saucepan. Beat egg yolks, milk and ½ cup wine with rotary beater; stir into gelatin mixture. Heat to boiling over low heat, stirring constantly. Chill in bowl of ice water, stirring occasionally, until mixture is room temperature, 3 to 5 minutes.

Mix 2 tablespoons wine and 1 cup wafer crumbs; stir into cooled mixture. Beat 1 cup cream in chilled small mixer bowl until stiff. Fold into gelatin-crumb mixture. Beat egg whites in small mixer bowl until stiff; fold into gelatin-crumb mixture. Spoon into crumb crust. Refrigerate until firm, at least 3½ hours.

Beat 1 cup cream and 3 tablespoons sugar in chilled small mixer bowl until stiff; spread on filling. Garnish with almonds. Refrigerate before serving.

Chocolate Pudding with Cinnamon Whip Topping

½ cup granulated sugar
⅓ cup cocoa
2 tablespoons cornstarch
⅛ teaspoon salt
1¾ cups milk
2 egg yolks, slightly beaten
¼ cup medium white wine
2 teaspoons vanilla
½ cup whipping cream
1 tablespoon medium white wine
¼ teaspoon ground cinnamon
1 tablespoon powdered sugar
¼ teaspoon vanilla

Mix granulated sugar, cocoa, cornstarch and salt in 2-quart saucepan. Stir in milk gradually. Heat to boiling over medium heat, stirring constantly. Boil and stir 1 minute.

Mix egg yolks and ¼ cup wine. Stir at least half of the hot mixture gradually into egg yolk mixture; stir back into hot mixture in pan. Boil and stir 1 minute. Remove from heat. Stir in 2 teaspoons vanilla. Pour pudding into 4 dessert dishes. Cool slightly; refrigerate until chilled.

Mix cream, 1 tablespoon wine and the cinnamon in small mixer bowl. Refrigerate 30 minutes. Stir in powdered sugar and ¼ teaspoon vanilla. Beat until soft mounds form; spoon onto pudding.

4 servings.

Lemon-Wine Torte

3 egg whites
¼ teaspoon cream of tartar
¾ cup sugar
¾ cup sugar
3 tablespoons cornstarch
¼ teaspoon salt
⅔ cup medium white wine
¼ cup water
3 egg yolks, slightly beaten
1 tablespoon butter or margarine
2 teaspoons grated lemon peel
¼ cup lemon juice
1 cup chilled whipping cream

Heat oven to 375°. Cover baking sheet with heavy brown paper. Beat egg whites and cream of tartar in small mixer bowl until foamy. Beat in ¾ cup sugar, 1 tablespoon at a time; continue beating until stiff and glossy. (Do not underbeat.)

On brown paper, shape meringue into 9-inch circle, building up side. Bake 1½ hours. Turn off oven; leave meringue in oven with door closed 1 hour. Remove from oven and finish cooling away from draft.

Mix ¾ cup sugar, the cornstarch and salt in 2-quart saucepan. Stir in wine and water gradually. Heat over medium heat, stirring constantly, until mixture thickens and boils. Boil and stir 1 minute. Remove from heat. Stir at least half of the hot mixture into the egg yolks gradually. Stir back into hot mixture in pan. Boil and stir 1 minute. Remove from heat; stir in butter, lemon peel and lemon juice. Cool to room temperature. Spoon into meringue shell. Refrigerate at least 12 hours.

Beat cream in chilled small mixer bowl until stiff; spread over filling. Garnish with shredded lemon peel if desired.

8 to 10 servings.

Wine Cream Roll

3 eggs
1 cup granulated sugar
⅓ cup water
1 teaspoon vanilla
1 cup cake flour or ¾ cup
    all-purpose flour*
1 teaspoon baking powder
¼ teaspoon salt
    Powdered sugar
⅓ cup granulated sugar
1 tablespoon plus 1 teaspoon cornstarch
1 cup dry white wine
2 eggs, slightly beaten
3 tablespoons butter or margarine
2 tablespoons cornstarch
1 package (10 ounces) frozen
    strawberries, thawed and drained
    (reserve 2 tablespoons syrup)
¾ cup currant jelly
1 tablespoon lemon juice

Heat oven to 375°. Line jelly roll pan, 15½x10½x1 inch, with aluminum foil; grease. Beat 3 eggs in small mixer bowl until very thick and lemon colored, about 5 minutes; pour into large mixer bowl. Beat in 1 cup granulated sugar gradually. On low speed, mix in water and vanilla. Add flour, baking powder and salt gradually, beating just until batter is smooth. Pour into pan, spreading batter to corners. Bake until wooden pick inserted in center comes out clean, 12 to 15 minutes.

Loosen cake from edges of pan; invert on towel sprinkled with powdered sugar. Remove foil; trim stiff edges if necessary. While hot, roll cake and towel beginning at a narrow end. Cool on wire rack.

Mix ⅓ cup granulated sugar and 1 tablespoon plus 1 teaspoon cornstarch in 2-quart saucepan. Stir in wine. Cook over medium heat, stirring constantly, until mixture thickens and boils. Boil and stir 1 minute. Stir half the mixture gradually into the eggs; stir back into mixture in pan. Boil and stir 1 minute. Remove from heat. Stir in butter. Refrigerate until chilled.

Unroll cake and remove towel. Spread filling over roll to within ¼ inch of edges; roll up. Refrigerate at least 1 hour.

Mix 2 tablespoons cornstarch and the reserved strawberry syrup. Heat strawberries and jelly to boiling in 1½-quart saucepan. Stir in cornstarch mixture. Heat to boiling, stirring constantly. Boil and stir 2 minutes. Remove from heat. Stir in lemon juice; cool. Serve with cake.

10 servings.

*If using self-rising flour, omit baking powder and salt.

Pound Cake à l'Orange

1 package (16 ounces) golden
   pound cake mix
½ cup granulated sugar
½ cup sweet white wine
½ teaspoon grated orange peel
½ cup orange juice
   Powdered sugar

Prepare cake as directed on package except—pour batter into greased and floured 9-cup bundt cake pan. Bake until wooden pick inserted in center comes out clean, 45 to 55 minutes.

While cake is cooling, mix granulated sugar, wine, orange peel and orange juice in 1½-quart saucepan. Heat to boiling, stirring constantly. Boil and stir 1 minute. Remove from heat.

Cool cake 5 minutes; remove from pan. Invert on serving plate. Pierce top of cake gently with fork, inserting tines as far as possible. Spoon syrup over cake; let stand until syrup is absorbed, about 30 minutes. Sprinkle top of cake with powdered sugar. Nice garnished with orange slices.

Honey-Lemon Cake

1 package (18.5 ounces)
   lemon cake mix with pudding
1 cup medium white wine
½ cup sugar
¼ cup honey
   Three 3-inch cinnamon sticks
3 whole cloves
1 cup chilled whipping cream
2 tablespoons honey
½ cup unflavored yogurt
   Diced roasted almonds

Bake cake in oblong baking pan, 13x9x2 inches, as directed on package.

While cake is baking, heat wine, sugar, ¼ cup honey, the cinnamon sticks and cloves to boiling in 1½-quart saucepan, stirring constantly; reduce heat. Simmer uncovered, stirring occasionally, 15 minutes; cool.

Cool cake 5 minutes. Cut into serving-size pieces. Remove cinnamon sticks and cloves from syrup. Pour syrup slowly over cake in pan; cool.

Beat cream and 2 tablespoons honey in chilled small mixer bowl until stiff. Fold in yogurt. Refrigerate until serving time. Serve cake with yogurt topping. Garnish with almonds.

Index